IT'S NEVER ABOUT WHAT IT'S ABOUT

IT'S NEVER ABOUT WHAT IT'S ABOUT

WHAT

WE

LEARNED

ABOUT

LIVING

WHILE WAITING TO DIE

KRANDALL KRAUS

PAUL BORJA

FOREWORD BY

ROBERT A. JOHNSON

alyson books
los angeles | new york

MANUFACTURED IN THE UNITED STATES OF AMERICA.

THIS TRADE PAPERBACK ORIGINAL IS PUBLISHED BY
ALYSON PUBLICATIONS,
P.O. BOX 4371, LOS ANGELES, CA 90078-4371.
DISTRIBUTION IN THE UNITED KINGDOM BY
TURNAROUND PUBLISHER SERVICES LTD.,
UNIT 3, OLYMPIA TRADING ESTATE, COBURG ROAD, WOOD GREEN,
LONDON N22 6TZ ENGLAND.

FIRST EDITION: AUGUST 2000

00 01 02 03 04 **a** 10 9 8 7 6 5 4 3 2 1

ISBN: 1-55583-571-6

LIBRARY OF CONGRESS CATALOGING-IN-PUBLICATION DATA
    KRAUS, KRANDALL.
       IT'S NEVER ABOUT WHAT IT'S ABOUT : WHAT WE LEARNED ABOUT
    LIVING WHILE WAITING TO DIE / KRANDALL KRAUS, PAUL BORJA ;
    FOREWORD BY ROBERT A . JOHNSON.—1ST ED.
          ISBN 1-55583-571-6
          1. CONDUCT OF LIFE. 2. DEATH—PSYCHOLOGICAL ASPECTS. 3. AIDS
    (DISEASE)—PATIENTS—CONDUCT OF LIFE. 4. KRAUS, KRANDALL.
    5. BORJA, PAUL. I. BORJA, PAUL. II.TITLE.
    BF637.C5 K73 2000
    155.9'37—DC21   00-026639

CREDITS
QUOTATIONS FROM *THE ENLIGHTENED MIND: AN ANTHOLOGY OF
    SACRED PROSE*, EDITED BY STEPHEN MITCHELL, ARE USED BY PERMIS-
    SION OF HARPERCOLLINS PUBLISHERS, NEW YORK. © 1991.
QUOTATIONS FROM *THE ENLIGHTENED HEART: AN ANTHOLOGY OF
    SACRED POETRY*, EDITED BY STEPHEN MITCHELL, ARE USED BY PER-
    MISSION OF HARPERCOLLINS PUBLISHERS, NEW YORK. © 1989.
"PLEASURE, HAPPINESS, AND JOY" APPEARED IN ISSUE #42 OF *WHITE
    CRANE: A JOURNAL EXPLORING GAY MEN'S SPIRITUALITY*.
COVER PHOTOGRAPHY AND DESIGN BY PHILIP PIROLO.

This work is dedicated with love and respect to Robert A. Johnson, Qi-Re Qing, Kim Storch, and Felix and Catalina Borja,

And in loving memory of
Elizabeth Farrell Kaiser

Contents

WE WOULD LIKE TO ACKNOWLEDGE:

Ron Baumhover, for reading and challenging our ideas, and keeping the house running;

Dr. Marge Poscher, for keeping us alive and well long enough to do the inner work;

Carol Yaggy and Mary Twomey for giving us the house in Anchor Bay where we wrote the rough draft;

David Marshall, whose artistic and technical contributions gave the book its original incarnation;

Andre Laventure, Rick Padgett, Pete Zimmerman, Clark Henley, and the countless others who have died of HIV Disease, for showing us how to die, and, more importantly, how to live until we do; and

Scott Brassart, who makes publishing almost as meaningful as writing.

Without the generous support of the following individuals we could never have succeeded in completing the publication of this book:

Anthony Turney; Mr. and Mrs. William Henley; Dr. Walter Krampf; Richard Woo; Arlene Joe; Daniel Andrade; James and Che Caldwell; Jill Visor; Randy and Vera Swanson; Debra Howard; Raul Montalvo; Paul Alley; John Holden; Jerry and Monica Filush; Josephine Jacbosen; Keith Schroeder/Castro Photo, San Francisco; Joan Bellefontaine; Garland Richard Kyle; Jean Bolen; Paula Grace; Catherine Lee; Marcia Freed; Ruth and Paul Workman; Alice Baer; Herta Glas; Carol Yaggy; Mary Twomey; Frank Gasparik; William Meredith; Richard Harteis; Debra Haber; Deborah J. Schmall.

You are about to read a book about dying and living—not a book about living and dying, but about dying and living. There is a difference—a tremendous difference. Once you have experienced dying, the experience of living is changed unalterably and forever. Nothing looks, sounds, or feels the same again. The world and all that is in it take on a translucent quality. One sees "through the world," as it were, into the heart of things. The trivial falls away, essences come to the surface; nothing is merely what it appears to be. Blustery men, provocative women, weeping children, even automobiles, trees, oceans, Fourth of July parades—all take on a kind of diaphanous quality.

It is as though you see not just the material thing itself but the energy within that makes each thing what it is. Perhaps it might be more specific to say it is as though you see the inner energy that makes each thing "act the way it does." This can be a terrible knowledge if one is not prepared to hold it respectfully. It is also a terrible knowledge if we try to control it. It is a wonderful knowledge if we can experience it with love and respect for what it really is: a mirror into the self. The wisdom that shines forth through that looking glass presents us an opportunity to serve the Self and, thereby, to serve others.

I made my peace early on with death, and my real problems after that have all been with life. At the age of 11 I was in a terrible automobile accident. After the doctors sewed my arteries together again I was confined in a plaster cast. In the middle of the night an artery broke loose and I began to bleed. An alert nurse found the blood seeping through the cast and whisked me off to surgery just in time to draw me back from...well, from where?

Quite simply, I had been dying. I had been drawn into a state that I can only very poorly describe as the purest peace, beauty, color, exaltation, joy, exuberance, and safety. Even these words in our sorely inadequate language cannot come near to conveying the experience.

As I was dying I was fully aware of what was happening. I was entering death in high consciousness. I resisted. I set my feet down like a mule and refused to go over the line from life to death, but finally I was drawn into the next world whether I agreed or not. It was at this time that I was entering surgery, and what the surgeon and his team of assistants were doing to me on the operating table dragged me back into life again. "Dragged" is the pertinent word, since I resisted coming back as vigorously as I had resisted entering into the next world.

It was difficult to live in the world again after that. Most people would probably describe the experience as a kind of "heavenly" experience, because the feelings were of being in a state of perfection. In the years that followed that event I slowly learned ways other than dying to contact that "heavenly world" I had previewed. My own books speak of the ways I found and make a chronicle of that journey. A careful reader will see that I never speak of anything else.

Once a person walks with death, nothing in this world can possibly be perceived in the same way. After such an experience, whether it is a "near-death" experience or the diagnosis of a terminal illness, the state of "non-death," or being in this world, is a difficult one in which to exist. But there is a way to live with it, and the way to live with it can be gleaned from the experience itself.

A good dream, like a good myth, will not only present our inner condition to our consciousness, it will also present the solution to the dilemma we face. So will coming face to face with death. No matter how we experience death's proximity, we cannot forget it. Whether we have the kind of near-death experience I had at age 11, actually entering into some "other world," or we simply look Death itself in the eye and escape with our lives, we can never forget the experience. It is indelibly etched in the psyche; and therein lies our solution: Never forget death.

The tendency for we mortals, however, is to try very hard to forget death. If our experience of coming close to death frightened us, we want to run far and fast from it; if it was a joyous event, then as time goes by we may begin to disbelieve it actually happened to us. "Perhaps," we tell ourselves, "it was all in my mind." (As if what is in our mind isn't real!)

And yet we can't forget it totally. It remains there, vivid and unforgettable, a powerful experience in our memory. Once we have come so close to death, try as we may to live life without thinking about death, we cannot. Like Lot's wife in the Old Testament story, we simply cannot help but turn and look back. We are drawn to the experience over and over after it happens. We find ourselves thinking of it, musing over it, interpreting it, even challenging its authenticity. No matter how we feel about the experience, we cannot help but keep thinking about it. That irresistible urge of the psyche to "look back," to keep an eye on death, is precisely the answer to handling the dilemma of living in the world. That haunting call to remember death is the solution to living consciously.

"Keep an eye on Death," we are often told. This is sage advice, but not for the reason most people think. When people say that they usually mean, "Don't let Death catch you." There is a far more satisfying and empowering reason for keeping an eye on Death. If we keep an eye on Death, we will be more conscious of life. One cannot help but notice the daylight if one has lived through the dark of night. Our first sight of gold is an extraordinary event if all we have ever seen is lead. A flower in our hand is a miracle if we have only touched withered grass. Yet in each case we must have both, for one defines the other.

So death keeps us alert to life and all its nuances, meanings and lessons. How can we truly appreciate life if we haven't walked with Death? And how do we keep an eye on Death, the guide to that other world, when it scares us so? How do we hold death in one hand, life in the other, and go on?

How to cope with death? The answer is simple—die. As Japanese Zen Master Maizumi Roshi says, "Why not die now and enjoy the rest of your life?" Not the death of our bodies, which will come in its own due time for everyone, but by the death which is our passport to the heavenly realm. It is the kind of death signified in the tarot by the Hanged Man: Change; turning your world upside down; dying to the ways of the outer world and being born to the ways of the inner world. We need not wait until our physical deaths to experience the joy that death ultimately brings. We can effect this change at any time.

Being modern people, we are mostly immune to the old ways of religious experience, but we possess an ability just as strong as some of the old rituals: the ability to love. Love is a language in and of itself. It is the language of that world beyond this one. Ask anyone who has had an experience such as the one I had at age 11. They will all tell you the same thing: The experience was one of overwhelming love.

If love is the language of heaven, it is a language we would do well to learn now. The language of love is an "inner language" that is heard in both the inner and the outer worlds. In loving ourselves, we comfort, nourish, nurture, encourage, and empower the best parts of our psyche. When we treat ourselves with such love and respect others are affected by it and want to participate in speaking this "language of love," this language that transcends the material world and effects marvelous transformations in and around us.

There is only one way to learn a language—and that is to practice it. The book you have in your hand is a good primer for that language. It speaks of dying, of living, and of loving. It takes us into the inner world, uses a simple language, and asks some basic questions. Take this language and practice it as often as possible. Speak it daily. You will grow proficient in no time.

Robert A. Johnson
Encinitas, California

The other day my partner Paul and I were out shopping in the neighborhood. As we were leaving one of the shops we witnessed an altercation on the sidewalk involving people calling each other the most hateful names—"nigger," "honky," "faggot," "breeder"—until we had to rush away from a scene we feared was about to erupt into physical violence.

Paul sighed and said to me, "We really ought to write a book. People just don't get it."

"What? What book?" I asked.

"People have all the epithets they want at their disposal: *nigger, faggot, kike, spic, bitch*. What they really need is an inner vocabulary," he said. "Most people seem spiritually illiterate. They don't see the poetry of living. They don't get the metaphors. We should write a book."

The more I thought about it, the more it sounded like a great project—fun, if nothing else. Another chance for Paul and me to do something intimate together that was also intellectually stimulating and challenging. But there was, of course, the problem of "credentials." Who are we to write a book that delves into the field of psychology when, even though both of us hold other degrees, we have no degrees in psychology. But a friend of ours blew a hole through that argument, saying, "What does it matter how many degrees you hold? What does it matter if you have three degrees or no degrees? Aristotle had no degree. Buddha didn't get his Bachelor of Arts. Shakespeare had no Ph.D. hanging on the wall of his study. Your credentials are your experience. Ten years of therapy are your experience. You're infected with the AIDS virus, for God's sake. You're dying! What more credentials does a person need to speak with authority about dying?"

We were convinced. Who cares who or what we are on paper, as long as we tell you something that assists in the daily toil of your life? Nothing grates me more than to read a magazine article or see a book cover or even receive a letter that is signed Mathilda Frankenstein, M.S.W., or Franklin Geoffrey Hoffenpfeffer, Ph.D. Oh, right, I wouldn't want to confuse the author with all those other Franklin Geoffrey Hoffenpfeffers—the ones who don't have a Ph.D. Please!

I decided that perhaps I should put my ego aside (thinking I always know what's best), and we should write the book after all. So I asked Paul if he would do it with me, since most of the fundamental principles came from our discussions, and because he is the only one I know who can help me think through tough concepts and articulate them. He's really the brains in the family. (And the brawn, too, come to think of it.) He agreed to coauthor with me, and we set to work.

Here, then, is the fruit of our labors. We strove to keep it simple, brief, to the point, and entertaining. You will have to be the judge of whether we succeeded.

To keep it simpler for the reader, we have written in the first person singular rather than the first person plural. We tried it in first person plural and there were sections that became grammatically confusing, if not impossible. So even though it is one voice you will find on the page, every word has been distilled by both of us. Paul practically dictated chapters five, eight, and 11 to me. In these areas I am but a novice.

CHAPTER ONE

REMEMBERING WHAT'S IMPORTANT

Have you ever been driving down the street on your way to some pleasant dinner date or on your way to work when suddenly someone in another car cuts you off or stops without warning and you abruptly explode with rage? You honk and scream and wave your hands around until the offending motorist is out of sight, then find yourself wishing him the most horrible of fates.

Or you're working busily in the kitchen or your office and as you go to move something you drop it—a stack of papers, a handful of chopped celery—and you simply lose control. You pick up the nearest object—a stapler, a saucer—and you hurl it to the floor or against the wall. You feel as if you're going to burst, you're so angry.

You're relaxing after a tiring day. Your feet are propped up on the coffee table. A big bowl of buttered popcorn rests in your lap. Your favorite old black-and-white movie is on, and you're deep into it. A commercial comes on for a long distance phone company, and it shows a young woman getting on a plane, leaving her parents for the first time. A few seconds later it shows the old couple at home on their front porch with their faithful dog.

Everyone is sad; they all miss the young woman. Then the phone rings and, of course, it's her, calling "just to say I love you." You burst into tears.

When that happens—and it happens to everyone sooner or later—do you ever ask yourself, "Where did all that emotion come from?" Probably you do, but just as probably you shrug your shoulders and move on, not in a very good mood, but moving on nonetheless. And of course, sooner or later, it happens again.

If you knew where all your anger came from, you might be able to get a handle on it. If you understood the source of your sorrow, perhaps you could hold it rather than have it come to the surface at the most unlikely times. We can all learn and accomplish a great deal regarding our "inner selves" in relation to our "outer behavior." But first we must see and understand that "it's never about what it's about."

Life would be so much more manageable if we had a few basic tools for understanding where certain feelings come from, especially the ones that make no sense to us. They can be feelings of rage or despair, the desire to kill, or a wish to run away. They are powerful feelings, and they can be insidious and dangerous; they pounce upon us and wreak havoc with our minds, not to mention our hearts.

They're not always our own feelings, either. Very often they are the feelings of others projected or thrown onto us in an attempt to get us to carry them. How many times have you been the victim of someone else? A coworker who always seems to attempt to undermine your efforts, make you look bad, sabotage your projects? A "friend" or relative who "plays with your head," making you feel inadequate as a friend, a wife, or a husband? A parent who tries to cast you in the light of an ungrateful child? Whether these feelings you carry are your own or someone else's, you end up becoming the victim. But once you have a way to understand what this behavior and these feelings really are and where they come from—that is, what they are *really* about—you can begin to liberate yourself from their menacing effects.

A GUIDING PRINCIPLE

In our house we have a principle that guides us through almost every facet of our lives. In fact, it's so pervasive that we've had matching T-shirts made with this principle, "It's Never About What It's About," written on them. We mean this quite literally. For us, it is the foundation of our individual lives, and it is the guiding principle of our relationship. From this basic guiding principle several other principles flow. They are fascinating, liberating, and enlightening.

These guiding principles are simple to understand, difficult to experience, and are observable throughout our entire society. Knowing what they are can change a person's life. Understanding them and how they work is liberating. Keeping them in consciousness is enlightening but definitely a 24-hour-a-day job; yet it's a job well worth the effort.

REMEMBERING WHAT'S IMPORTANT

A funny thing happens when you're dying. Not ha-ha–funny, but ironic-funny, peculiar-funny. When you know you're going to die soon, you finally begin to live. When time becomes short you cut out the extraneous activities, stop spending time with people who aren't "friends of virtue," and grow increasingly intolerant of people whining about petty annoyances. Suddenly you experience life as a wondrous place, an awesome time, a rare opportunity to know yourself and the universe around you.

In my experience people diagnosed with a terminal illness fall into two categories. The first group wakes up and begins doing the excruciatingly difficult work of finding out who they are and how to make the rest of their lives meaningful. The second group runs like hell. They stick their heads farther into the sand; they take their disability checks on the first of the month and head for the corner bar; they get mean and nasty and selfish and hurtful. More times than not those in the second group of people are just carrying to the extreme the personality traits they exhibited either openly or just beneath the surface for most of their lives.

The people I was close to who died of AIDS didn't "find themselves" until after their diagnoses. Most of them were tripping through life acting like the rest of us: as though we will never die. Then, when the message got delivered—"Not only are you going to die, but you're going to die very soon,"—most of these people began cleaning up what was left of their lives. They got sober, stopped abusing drugs, engaged family and friends in a healing process, and worked hard at making bad relationships good again. They became more selfless, more emotionally available, and more spiritually developed. Not everyone does this, mind you. I've been lucky to know some very courageous people.

My late partner Andre was somewhat of an exception to begin with. He was spiritually developed at the age of 24 when I met him. I don't know how he accomplished that, but who and what he was got me to start thinking that reincarnation may be a fact. There was no other way to explain him. He came from an abusive home and dropped out of high school before his senior year. I believe he must have brought his wisdom with him from previous lives.

My current partner and I are examples of people who were green but looking to be fully ripe. We both had spent many years of our lives searching for some meaning. Paul had been in the seminary and was much more actively involved in a spiritual and intellectual life than I was when we met. I was more of a disillusioned former party boy. But I was searching. Andre had introduced me to meditation and I had been practicing it on and off for 12 years. When Paul and I met we complemented each other's spiritual and intellectual quests. We were also trying to understand ourselves emotionally. Both of us had lost partners; both of us were infected with the AIDS virus. We were filled with sorrow and rage, and we hadn't a clue what to do with the feelings.

Although we were both HIV positive, we were healthy. But about two years after moving in together we each began to exhibit symptoms. When that happened we figured time was drawing to a close for us. Paul left his job, taking disability; I went on disability a few months after that. By winter of 1996 we felt as if maybe we had a year or two left. We increased our time with each other, spending our days working in the garden or going to the movies. In the evening after dinner we would read to each other. I took up crocheting and began making afghans for the friends I was about to leave behind so they would have something personal from me, something soft, warm, and loving to remind them of me and how I loved them.

We started doing volunteer work and formed an AIDS support group. We prayed every day at least twice: once in the morning, separately, and then in the afternoon we would sit together for prayer and meditation. We found ourselves spending more time with our women friends and supporting others in the struggles they had in relationships and with jobs. We were quiet and peaceful and content. We often commented to each other how ironic it was that now that we were dying we'd never felt more alive. And while we were much more reclusive, we were more attuned to the world and more in love with each other than ever before.

REMEMBERING WHO WE ARE

Then the universe threw a monkey wrench into things. Along came protease inhibitors, a new kind of drug that spurred profound effects on people with HIV, causing in some a complete disappearance of the virus. Because our health was failing so quickly our physician managed to get us into a clinical trial. The first three weeks were difficult adjustment periods for both of us, and for a while we thought we might have to stop the medications. Then, just when it looked as if we couldn't take it any longer, our side effects disappeared and the drug began to work. Each of us improved dramatically.

I became more involved with my AIDS work at the state level; Paul went back to the gym and brought his body to a level of health and stamina unlike any he'd ever had—even before he was diagnosed. I finished a new novel, began work on two new books, and started running again. Both of us began spending more time with friends and acquaintances, traveling, going out to lunch and dinner, attending parties, and socializing in general. And the more we became engaged in life in the "outside world," the world of the "not-dying-soon," the more we found we didn't have time for some of the other things.

Sometimes a day or two or four or five would go by without us sitting for afternoon prayer. There were days when our schedules were so busy we hardly saw each other. When I traveled for the state we spent long hours on the phone and became aware that we communicated, if not better, certainly more directly, when I was out of town. What was happening to us? I remembered a story that shed light on what Paul and I were going through.

There is a common urban myth that haunts me and reminds me of Paul's and my experience. It seems there was a woman with a three-year-old son. She and her husband had just had another baby and the three-year-old was totally enamored of the new infant. Within days of bringing the baby home from the hospital the three-year-old began imploring his mother to let him hold the baby. Then a few days after that he began asking if he could be alone with the baby in the baby's room. The mother thought it was cute, but of course declined the request. The baby was too fragile to be left in the care of a three-year-old child.

For the next few weeks the woman's son continued asking his mother if he could just be alone for a few minutes with his new baby sister. The asking grew into begging and begging became a frantic pleading. The woman was growing concerned. What was it that her son wanted? She and her husband had tried very hard to make sure they didn't slight their son after the new baby was born. Was he jealous? Did he intend to harm the baby? What was this all about?

At last the mother consulted a child psychologist. The psychologist suggested that the woman allow her son time with the child, but to make certain everything was all right, she also suggested installing a listening device to monitor the baby's room. That way if anything untoward happened, she could intervene. The mother took the woman's advice, and after installing the device she told her son he could spend time alone with the baby. She took her son into the baby's room and left, closing the door behind her. As she closed the door she saw her son standing at the crib but looking at her as if to make sure she was closing the door and leaving them in private.

The mother rushed into her own bedroom and clicked on the listening device, and this is what she heard: "Quick, tell me about God. I'm starting to forget."

Paul and I decided to write this book because we don't want to forget what we learned about living while we were waiting to die. We don't want to slip back into denial; we don't want to lose sight of our mortality. In other words, we want to remember who we really are.

We must stay with death if we are to be death's friend; or more precisely, if death is to be our friend. If we are to have fully meaningful lives, if we are to know the wholeness and the goodness of being, we must never forget all that we learned when we were within sight of death's door.

Paul and I are trying to slow down now. We are trying to remember, trying to experience that we are living *and* dying. We are trying to live life with our minds, hearts, souls, and senses fully open.

There is an ancient Hindu formula for a perfect life and the attainment of bliss: Every moment, think of God and remember your own death. We think it is sage wisdom. We suggest it for everyone.

CHAPTER TWO

IT'S NEVER ABOUT WHAT IT'S ABOUT

One morning not long ago I was washing the breakfast dishes. I was almost finished when I remembered there was still a dirty frying pan on the stove, so I turned to get it. What I didn't realize, however, was that while I had been standing at the sink my dog Hari had come into the kitchen and curled up behind me. When I turned and started to walk toward the stove, I tripped over him and nearly fell to the floor. Only reaching out and grabbing the refrigerator kept me from taking a nasty tumble.

After I recovered my footing I saw the dog and began screaming at him at the top of my lungs. Naturally Hari had no idea what he had done wrong, and when he saw my rage he fled the scene, which made me even angrier. Now, I have lived with dogs my entire life and I have never struck one. I simply don't believe in it and have learned it isn't necessary. The tone of one's voice is the only cue a dog needs to understand whether he has pleased you or displeased you; but that morning I wanted to hit him. I reached into the dish drainer as he scampered from the room, grabbed a mug and threw it—not at Hari, but at the floor. It shattered, and I stood there looking at what I had done as though I had just woken up from sleepwalking.

THE FIRST QUESTION:

I have tripped over dogs for thirty years. For as long as I can remember, there has been a dog or a cat somewhere in the house and they're forever in the way. I high-step, sidestep, even hop sometimes, to avoid colliding with them. But this particular day I did none of those things. This particular morning I was mentally distracted. I stepped back, tripped, became instantly enraged, and instinctively struck out. Why?

After finding Hari and reassuring him that he had nothing to fear from me, I sat in the living room and discussed the event with my partner, Paul. I find that most often, if I have someone to talk with, Truth emerges more quickly. The first question Paul and I thought needed answering was this:

Was my reaction to what happened a reasonable response?

Clearly the answer was "No." Smashing dishes out of blind rage simply because I tripped over my pet, whom I love and feel protective of, is at the very least an overreaction. So where did that anger come from?

THE SECOND QUESTION:

Was there something in the recent past that might have been on my mind?

I reconstructed the previous few days in an attempt to get to the root of the problem. This is what I came up with:

I am a member of a statewide advisory body called the

California Comprehensive Care Working Group. We make recommendations to the governor on how to allocate the money the federal government gives to the state of California to provide health services to people with HIV disease. This year had been particularly difficult because new drugs have come onto the scene resulting in amazing changes in people's health, but the drugs are horribly expensive. One way these drugs are made available to people without insurance is through a state-operated program called ADAP, the AIDS Drug Assistance Program.

It became clear long before we added the new drugs to the list that the program was going to run out of money before the end of the fiscal year. For one thing, more people were signing up for medications under ADAP than ever before. Now the Working Group was recommending to the governor that the new drugs, called protease inhibitors, be added to the list of medications available through ADAP. The state department of finance, which always wants budget justifications for every expenditure, was blocking our attempt. They said we had to prove that adding the new drugs wouldn't bankrupt the fund. That, of course, was not possible because adding the new drugs would definitely cost more than was currently allocated to the program. In order to add the drugs we would also need to add more money to the budget, something the department of finance and the governor were not interested in doing.

For months I had been part of an effort to get the governor to take money out of the state general fund and put it into ADAP. The evening before the dog incident I received a telephone call from Sacramento informing me that the governor was refusing to contribute any more money to the fund and was planning on taking money away from other AIDS programs in order to add the drugs to the ADAP list. In other words, the State was planning on "robbing Peter to pay Paul." That meant that the people with AIDS who were the most sick and required home health care would not get the services they needed so that others who were not so sick might get the medications needed to prevent their disease from progressing. I was outraged.

But there was nothing anyone could do at this point. We had exhausted all avenues. Even shouting and screaming and throwing things at the governor wasn't going to help. So I held this anger and frustration in. That is, until I tripped over Hari.

So the answer to the first question was "No, my reaction to tripping over the dog was not a reasonable response." It was far more extreme than was appropriate. No one in his or her right mind has that reaction to tripping over a dog.

The answer to the second question was, "A lot of frustrating things have been going on lately that I haven't been able to express my anger and frustration about. This was obviously connected to that."

But the reaction was so "blind," so enraged, so automatic. What's more, the feeling was so violent that it frightened not only the dog but me too. What was that violent reaction really about? What triggered it? What button was being pushed?

THE THIRD QUESTION:

What was the exact feeling at the moment I tripped?

Figuring out the answer to this question was extremely difficult. My first thought was that I felt anger, but upon reflection I realized that my anger came after I regained my balance. So what was the feeling at the very instant I tripped? Reliving the moment in my mind got me right to it. At the very moment I was falling I was afraid. I felt panic, overwhelmed with sudden fear.

At the moment I was losing my balance I felt out of control. I was definitely afraid. Not easy to admit in our society, especially for men, but there it was and I was admitting it.

But afraid of what? Now the process got really complex and murky. When I asked myself the question "What was I afraid of?" and just listed whatever came to mind, I produced the following:

I was afraid of hurting the dog.

I was afraid of hurting myself.

I was afraid of losing control.

I was afraid of being in a situation the outcome of which was uncertain.

Fear around all of those situations seems perfectly natural to me. Who wouldn't be afraid of those things? But the process became more difficult and more uncomfortable when I got to the next question that Paul and I decided needed to be asked. It took me to a somewhat deeper level of my psyche.

THE FOURTH QUESTION:

Have I ever felt this same feeling before?

Upon reflection I found that my answer was "Yes, plenty of times." I could even list a few of them, and once I did they made up a most curious collection of events:

Last winter when I fell down the back steps.

Every time Paul sneezes.

When my previous partner told me his HIV test came back positive.

This was indeed a strange group of seemingly unrelated events. My being afraid was the only thing the events had in common. As uncomfortable as it felt, I knew I had to go deeper. Besides, now my curiosity was stirred.

How complex do our simplest actions and reactions really get? How deep is the ocean of the unconscious, and how often do I have no idea of why I do and say certain things? I really wanted some answers, no matter how uncomfortable the process was. Paul and I took a break. I went running, he went to the gym, and we continued our discussion over supper.

Going beyond ground level with a dilemma such as this is always difficult for a variety of reasons. I believe the primary reason it's so tough is because it requires us to evoke memories and feelings we don't want to reexperience. Yet without going to the deep level where the reasons for our actions exist, we remain doomed to repeat those actions over and over.

We hear the term *acting out* used a lot these days. In my outburst at the dog we have a classic example of what it means. When we have feelings that are disturbing and we don't turn our attention inward to where the feelings are coming from, we end up "acting out" the feelings in ways that have little or nothing to do with the real problem. This acting out is confusing. It confuses and frightens the people around us, and sometimes it even confuses and frightens ourselves.

Our pouting, shouting, sulking, and stomping don't correlate with the visible issue at hand—like my tripping over the dog. Imagine how perplexed an observer would have been watching me scream at the dog and throw dishes just because I had nearly stepped on him.

Acting out always backfires, if only because we end up feeling worse when we're through. Not only that, but acting out can turn extremely ugly in no time. Eventually throwing dishes may turn into striking others or even doing physical damage to ourselves.

Some classic examples of acting out that we see all around us come immediately to mind: alcoholism, drug abuse, sexual promiscuity, all kinds of juvenile delinquency. Each one can be a convenient, though desperate, way to let out—or repress—strong feelings that have been bottled up inside for a long time. When the rage is strong enough anything is possible.

I had to admit that my anger wasn't about Hari; my anger was about something else. It seemed most likely that it was about my failed attempts to get the governor to increase the state budget for people with HIV disease in California. I was as angry about this as I have ever been about anything in my life. More friends and acquaintances of mine have died from AIDS than I can count—literally. It is a terminal illness; it is contagious; and now, for the first time since the epidemic began, we have a group of medications proven effective in making most people with HIV disease feel better and live longer. How on earth could anyone with even an ounce of compassion say no to funding these drugs? I just didn't understand.

I was angry, and other than standing around ranting about it with my other angry friends, there was no way to express my anger—certainly no adequate way. I couldn't get into the governor's office to yell at him. That might have helped a little, but even that could never begin to dissipate the amount of rage inside me.

Our society doesn't allow people to express anger. We aren't taught from an early age how to hold feelings of anger. No one shows us appropriate, healthy ways to express it. We're trained in lots of other ways: which side of the plate our fork goes on, how to tie our shoes, and how to put our toys back where we got them. But expressions of anger are discouraged and almost always punished. Any child who dares to "throw a tantrum" is immediately sent to his room or worse. As a society we simply aren't equipped to deal with anger. It frightens us.

So tripping over Hari scared me. Being scared made me even angrier. It triggered not only the anger at the dog for being in my way, but also released the anger I had been unable to express at the governor. As is often the case, especially with men, fear begets anger, which begets more fear. It can easily become a never-ending chain of emotions that sometimes can only be broken from the outside.

Getting at feelings that lie near the surface is only part of the work. The real issues lie somewhere even deeper, and getting to them is essential for understanding one's self as well as for developing the ability to manage strong feelings and keep them from getting out of control. When our emotions get out of control—whether it's anger or infatuation—we act hastily and often foolishly, only to pay a severe price later. We might kill someone or marry a person we can never love. But if we can know what the feelings really are about when they occur, perhaps we can keep ourselves from acting out inappropriately and paying for it later.

So now I knew I had to go deeper. I had to go farther back to find the things that were triggering such violent, frightening reactions in me.

THE FIFTH QUESTION:

Can I remember the very first time I felt that way?

It's easy to miss the mark a few times with this question. Sometimes I even try to fool myself. Every time I engage in this exercise I almost always begin by telling myself, "I never felt that way before."

Next I usually decide it was just a short while back that I first felt like this, perhaps one of the instances I listed when I was answering the second question. But eventually, if I'm courageous enough, I will go all the way back to my childhood. In this particular instance the farthest back I could go with this feeling was when my first dog, Corky, accidentally got out of the house one day and was run over by a lumber truck in the small Northern California town where I grew up.

I came home from school and found him curled up in the closet, his left front leg badly crushed. My father's only words to me were, "Did you leave the screen door unlocked?" I told him I hadn't, but it was clear that he was angry and that he thought I was the one responsible. He never accused me (he too was never taught how to express his anger appropriately), so I never had the opportunity to defend myself. I was at school when the dog got out, so I couldn't have been responsible. But from that day on it felt as if I were the one to blame, and there was never anything I could do to prove my innocence.

It was a scenario that would be played out over and over between me and my father throughout my life. I was always doing something wrong; I was never quite good enough; I was to blame for all the bad things that happened in our family. It was never stated quite like that but that's how it felt. It seemed obvious to me that I was our family's biggest problem, at least in the eyes of my father. So I never fully belonged, never felt accepted.

The odd irony of growing up in this neurotic condition was that when I discovered I was gay and was feeling different from everyone else and clearly on the outside of society, it was a feeling I was familiar with. In fact, it was a feeling I quickly learned to handle. It never changed the isolation, the sadness, or the fear that comes with being gay in a society that doesn't consider homosexuality acceptable, but it did toughen me.

My father walked around for months in a visible rage about the dog's medical bills and about having to take special care of him: carrying him up and down the steps, changing his bandages, taking him to the vet every week or two for checkups. My father, however, would never say anything about it directly.

Meanwhile, I slept in the closet every night with Corky, crying myself to sleep with my arms around my wounded cocker spaniel puppy. I was filled with remorse, guilt, and fear. I was afraid he would die and I would lose my best and only friend. Then I would have to face my father alone. Since I had no brothers or sisters, all attention would focus on me. When something went wrong my father would have only me to blame. *And why shouldn't he?* I reasoned. After all, he thought I was the one who left the door open and was responsible for hurting the dog. And my father—like all grown-ups in the eyes of children— was smart and always right. Adults even tell their children this to make sure everyone is clear about who's the boss: "Adults always know what's best."

So I began to doubt myself. Maybe I did leave the door open and didn't remember. Maybe somehow it was my fault. Maybe there was something wrong with me after all. (Looking back on it as an adult with a clearer understanding of my father, I find myself wondering how much of his anger was about the dog being hurt, how much of it was about the veterinary bills, and how much of it went back to his own childhood.) Finally Corky's leg was amputated, and to this day, although I know I was not the one to leave the screen door unlocked, I feel as though I was somehow to blame.

When I think of my childhood dog I can't help but think of him limping through the rest of his life, and when I think of that I feel my father's rage. I also reexperience my frustration at his passive-aggressive accusations and my own helplessness: I couldn't prove my innocence, and there was nothing I could do to make Corky's life easier. Although I loved the dog tremendously I never looked at him without feeling great sadness at his plight. He was different from every other dog in the neighborhood—in the whole world, for all I knew. He could never chase a rabbit or a ball, could never run, could never jump up on the sofa. There were times when I looked into his eyes and saw his own frustration and sadness at his less than dog-like existence. Later, I would feel exactly the same way when I realized I was attracted to other boys and was (or so I felt) different from every other boy in the neighborhood—in the whole world, for all I knew. And there wasn't a thing I could do about that either.

These feelings of sadness, helplessness, fear, guilt, and even my father's rage were all the same feelings I felt in the moment I tripped over Hari. They all came flooding back to me in that one instant. But what about those other things I listed when I was answering the second question?

Last winter when I fell down the back steps.

Last winter, as I fell down the stairs in the dark I thought I was about to incur some terrible bodily damage. I was in a state of panic as I tumbled down the concrete steps, feeling stupid for tripping, afraid of what parts of my body would break or bruise, and angry that I had been so clumsy. Along with all those feelings were a good dose of guilt and a lot of shame at being such an oaf.

Every time Paul sneezes.

The most curious one on that list was "every time Paul sneezes." When Paul sneezes I am immediately overcome with rage, no matter when or where or why he sneezes. After working long and hard to remember the first time I had those feelings, I realize now why those feelings come up. When I was a young boy my father used to get drunk every Saturday and Sunday without fail. He would either go to the local bar and spend the day with his buddies watching some sports event on television or he would putter around in the garage all day, drinking beer after beer.

By the time he came to the dinner table at 6 o'clock he was sloppily and disgustingly drunk, and sooner or later, before he either stumbled to bed or passed out at the table, he would go into a sneezing fit. This happened only when he got drunk, but it happened every time. He would sneeze and sneeze and sneeze, unable to stop sometimes for five or ten minutes. I would sit and watch, helpless to do anything about it. I couldn't make him stop sneezing any more than I could make him stop drinking and wreaking havoc on our weekends. I would usually end up leaving the supper table. I would go to my room, where I would cry or beat the mattress with my fists until my mother came and got me and the two of us would finish our meal alone, both of us confused, sad, and angry.

When my previous partner told me his HIV test came back positive.

Of course, when Andre was dying, I felt overwhelmingly sad. I could do nothing to stop the progression of the disease. No one could. When he died I would be left alone, and when I thought of that I felt a rush of panic go through my body. It made me angry that he was dying and I was helpless to stop it, but at whom could I be angry?

MAKING THE CONNECTION

So what did these events and the feelings that went along with them have to do with tripping over Hari? It made no sense. Feelings seldom do make sense, but we have them nonetheless. Paul, with more distance from the feelings, was able to help me find my way through the forest of emotions.

I was feeling helpless at my inability to rescue the ADAP program. I felt guilty that I couldn't do more, that I wasn't smart enough or clever enough or persuasive enough to change the governor's mind. I was afraid for the people who wouldn't be able to get the medications they needed, afraid that I might be one of them, afraid that Paul might be one of them, afraid that we would die.

I was sad that people with HIV are in such a sorry, unjust, and compassionless state of affairs. And, of course, I was enraged that people with a terminal illness literally have to take to the streets, engage in massive lobbying efforts, and demonstrate in front of the state capitol in order to get the medical care they need just to stay alive a little longer. These were all the same feelings I had about my father's injustice regarding Corky's injury and his drinking.

When I tripped over Hari it acted as a kind of trigger that fired the bullet of emotions. This bullet is filled with fear, frustration, guilt, anger, and sadness. It lives in the chamber of the gun that is my deep memory and sits waiting for some event—related or unrelated—to pull the trigger so the feelings can be released.

So my anger at tripping over Hari was not about tripping over Hari. It was about my failure with the ADAP program. It was about a lifetime of living with feelings of inadequacy, guilt, rage, and sadness. It was about my father's injustice, his lack of caring about my feelings, and his inability or refusal to empathize. Authority figures—presidents, senators, generals, governors—are, metaphorically speaking, "father figures." Naturally, the feelings came flooding in, along with self-recriminations: If only I were smarter; if only I had tried harder; if only I had thought of some approach no one else has ever thought of…. And on and on. All the same thoughts and feelings my father could spark in me with a single glance.

Just as when my father implied I had caused my puppy's injury, I was beginning to doubt myself, feel as if I had done something wrong or not done something I should have, even though I know now that is not true. So throwing the mug was really about an entire lifetime of feelings toward my father that never got expressed because no one ever taught me how to express them.

There is a long list of emotions that society has shoved into the shadows, out of the light, where they can't be seen; but like the wind, which also can't be seen, they can be quite distinctly felt. Sometimes the wind of these feelings is like a hurricane, and while we cannot see the wind itself, its effects are most visible and catastrophic. The feelings and actions we have shoved into the shadows are simply not acceptable to express in public—and perhaps not even in private. Those feelings in me were sitting there waiting for an opportunity to come raging forth.

CHAPTER THREE

THE PEOPLE INSIDE: MEETING OUR INNER SELVES

Before we can know how to proceed in the realm of the psyche we need to understand a few essential things about it. What I am about to say here is a terrible simplification—not to mention bastardization—of some very complex and fine work by the leading masters of psychology. But for our purposes we must word things in ordinary language, and this is my attempt at that. Because I am primarily a storyteller, I will be trying to explain things by telling stories and using anecdotes and analogies.

A few years ago one of our dogs, Axel, had some health problems. He was having trouble controlling his bladder. Nothing terribly messy, but he dribbled urine from time to time, especially in his sleep. We took him to the vet for tests. One of them was a water deprivation test, during which he had to be deprived of water for up to 48 hours. The objective of the test was to get him to concentrate his urine, which he had been unable to do for several days. He never did concentrate the urine, and they decided to perform another test to determine if the problem was in the brain or the kidneys. If the problem was in the brain, they could treat it with medication; if it was in the kidneys, there would be nothing they could do about it. We had to wait a week for the test results.

During this weeklong waiting process I was extremely distraught. I was depressed, anxious, sleepless, and distracted. My partner Paul was wonderfully supportive about it and let me have all my feelings without trying to force me out of my sadness, a very loving and difficult thing to do.

Many people comment from time to time about how "our pets are our children." I have never thought a lot about it other than to note that in my case I never thought of Axel as a child, and I don't think of our current dogs as children. I think of my dogs as dogs and they are pretty much treated as such. Granted, they are spoiled in some ways, but the ways seem rather benign: they get attention 99% of the time they seek it; they have a blanket we put on the sofa so they can escape the drafty floor of our old Victorian flat in cold weather. But they eat only dry dog food, except for table scraps, which are fed to them only in their bowl, never from the table. So it has always seemed to me that they are treated affectionately and, as Paul would say, as members of the family, but not like human beings.

What then was the reason for my strong empathetic response to Axel's situation? I've been thinking about this a lot, and there are some intriguing associations which shed light on it.

A BRIEF DIGRESSION

In Eastern spirituality one often comes across the statement, "Everything is a projection of your own mind." In the *Tibetan Book of the Dead*, Tibetan Buddhists advise us to remember this at the moment of our death, when both peaceful and wrathful deities appear before us and beckon us one way or the other. When we confront the ogres and frightening beings who are scaring us, rather than running away from them and ending up being reborn in the material world, the Tibetans advise us to tell ourselves "This is a projection of my own mind."

Once we realize this, recognition and liberation from the cycle of death and rebirth are simultaneous. In my student days my friends and I lumped this kind of thinking with the philosophical school of the skeptics. We always took great pleasure in pointing out that while a skeptic will tell us that the door isn't really there and that it is just a projection of our own mind, he will always open it before leaving the room.

But lately, with my new and deeper experience of Eastern ways, I understand the statement "Everything is a projection of your own mind" in a new light. It is not that the external world does not exist; it does, or it may, or it doesn't. That is not the point. The point is that the projection we make onto things, which determines their "reality" for us, is the value we place upon them. By *value* I do not mean only what we think a thing is worth in the material world, but rather the emotional, spiritual, and psychological interpretation we give things.

So one way of understanding the concept that "everything is a projection of our own minds" is to understand that the meaning we give to things (including people) is projected from our own minds. Let me give an example.

A HYPOTHETICAL EXAMPLE

I have grown up in this culture believing that one of the most important qualities of a human being is one's physical appearance. I dare say that holding beauty as a value is true of the vast majority of modern civilization, and while the aesthetic principles change from culture to culture, this principle seems to hold true around the world: beauty, however it is defined within a culture, is highly desirable. As a result, we are biased toward beautiful people. We want to be near them, to look at them, to touch them, to reward them for being beautiful, as though it were some kind of accomplishment they have striven to achieve. In other words, physical beauty is a value for most human beings. It connotes wholeness, harmony, integration, balance, and exhilaration: all the things that make us feel inflated, larger than life, and better than we normally feel about ourselves.

So upon boarding a busy city bus, if there are only two seats to be had, one next to a beautiful blonde woman with large breasts and curvaceous hips and a classical bone structure to her face, dressed in a stylish suit, and another seat next to an old crone with a hooked nose, dry, scraggly brown hair, no discernible figure, wearing a drab brown coat, most people will sit next to the blonde—because the value we project onto the blonde woman with the attractive body is a value with which we want to be associated. Beauty and all its associated attributes is a value we want for ourselves, and so we try to get close to beauty, hoping some will rub off on us and we too will be perceived as beautiful—which will help us to perceive ourselves as valuable.

We imagine the blonde woman is on her way to an audition for a role in a movie or meeting her executive boyfriend at his office. Perhaps she is going to try out for a part in a play or for the lead soprano role in an opera. Wherever she is headed, we are sure she will be met by other beautiful, successful people and whatever she is going to do will be done successfully. Surely when we part today, she will go on to live "happily ever after."

We look around the bus and take in the passengers. A young schoolboy carrying a leather bookbag brimming with books and papers sits gazing out the window. We assume he comes from a well-to-do family, sings in the church choir, will go on to have a successful career as a lawyer or a physician. He is clearly, at this age, a veritable angel of innocence.

There is also on the bus an elderly, white-haired man with a cane. He wears a suit and chats amiably with the woman next to him. We imagine him to be a kindly grandfather on his way to meet a friend for lunch. He has retired from a long career, perhaps owned his own business. A widower now, he lives with his children, helping them make ends meet with the income he earns from a lifetime of wise investments. Every evening he reads to his grandchildren by the fire and helps his daughter with the dinner dishes.

Behind him sits another man, overweight, wearing work pants and a denim jacket. He carries a lunch pail, which he has placed on the seat next to him so no one else can sit there and disturb him while he reads the sports page. His boots are caked with mud, and he is scowling at whatever it is he is reading in the newspaper, shaking his head from time to time in disgust. We are sure he is a surly and disagreeable man, mean to his wife, yells at his children when he comes home from his day's labor. He tells dirty jokes that are demeaning to women and minorities, shouts "faggot" at gay men who walk past where he works, and refers to co-workers as "niggers" and "spics." It is so clearly evident to us that we turn away in disgust.

Each person we see on the bus has a story, a history, and a personality, all of which we make up ourselves, some of it unconsciously, based upon what we observe of them as they ride to their destinations on this city bus. We have spoken to none of them, have watched no one perform any actions whatsoever; yet we ride along certain that we know what they're like inside. We project upon each of them an image or persona, but it all comes from inside us, not from the individuals themselves. Angelic Youth, Good Father, Cruel Barbarian, and so on. We have an entire storehouse of images or archetypes ready to project. All from inside ourselves.

THE POWER OF PROJECTION

Let's say we continue on this bus trip for a few blocks and at one point, as the bus turns to cut through the park, the blonde we've chosen to sit next to stands up, pulls out a gun, and tells everyone to put their wallets and money into a bag she throws at someone and orders to be passed around the bus.

Now we have a very different perception of this woman and so we probably will have a very different projection. She has done something we don't approve of, so we project evil and all its associated values onto her. Physically she hasn't changed a bit from when we first saw her when we boarded, but our projection has changed drastically. She has changed in our minds from Venus, Goddess of Love, to Kali, Wrathful Bitch. When we first saw her she was probably contemplating what she was about to do and just waiting for the right opportunity. Not knowing that, we projected a "positive" value onto her because of how beautiful she was. Now she has done something reprehensible, so we project a "negative" value onto her and have all the feelings that we connect with that negative value.

As the bus hits a bump the old crone across the aisle leaps up and grabs the woman's gun. It fires, and the old woman slumps to the floor fatally wounded. Now our perception of the physically unattractive woman has changed again, and we project a positive value onto her, one associated with courage, compassion, and virtue. "Why are you doing this?" the old woman asks the blonde, as she breathes her last. "Why?" The blonde, shaken now, begins to explain, almost to apologize. "I can't find work. My child is sick and needs medicine. I have no insurance. He'll die if I don't do something. I'm sorry."

Now we see the blonde woman in yet a different light. We take pity on her and sympathize with the difficult position she is in, for in our culture, sacrifice for one's children is one of the highest values. She is surely a victim of years of horrible discrimination, abuse, or cruelty. If it were later discovered that the old woman, whom we thought had risked and lost her life for the bus passengers, was in fact about to rob the bus herself and was trying to get the gun away from the blonde in order to commandeer the bus, our projections onto her would change again. We could go on and on with this example, but the point is that for every piece of information we take in, we assign a value of some sort, and it affects our response to the person, thing, or situation.

Very often we don't have much information at all, just a perception, such as how someone looks, as in the case of the passengers on the bus. We project onto others, sometimes without any reliable data, certain values that come from inside us, and these values are the most real part of life to us. These values are the motivations for how we live and act most of our lives. They may be triggered by how a person looks, what a person does, something a person says. Whatever the case, one thing remains constant—the value we project comes from inside us, and each one is loaded with feelings.

On the bus we were drawn to the blonde because we worship beauty. We adored our own doting, generous grandfather, so the old man seemed nothing but kind and sweet. We looked at the ugly old crone and recalled the nasty witch in *The Wizard of Oz* or the cruel stepmother in *Hansel and Gretel*, so we had feelings of disgust toward her. The young boy appeared just like depictions we have seen of a cherub at the throne of God, so we valued him as innocence itself. All of this is common. It goes on every day all around us and inside us.

How many of us have fallen in love with someone at first sight, only to break up a few weeks later, when we begin taking back our projections and seeing the person in his or her true light? A friend of mine recently fell in love and moved in with a beautiful young man. Eight months later, after finally discovering that the fellow was a pathological liar and was having psychotic breaks from reality, it was a virtual nightmare getting the guy out of the house and protecting my friend's pets and valuables. During the long process of getting the boyfriend to move out my friend kept asking over and over "How could I have made such a mistake?" One of the possible answers is that he projected upon the young man all the characteristics and qualities of his "ideal lover," his archetypal lover, before he even got to know the fellow. Sometimes falling in love with someone isn't about the beloved at all; it's about wanting to be in love. *It's never about what it's about!*

Jungian scholars will cringe at this simplistic presentation, but I am a layman trying to make sense out of the difficult and complex theories of scholarly psychology. I am trying to make useful the things I learned through my own experience and bring this science down to a decipherable level so people like me can make use of it in their daily lives. This is the only way I know to do that: to tell my story and simplify it in the most concrete terms possible. My apologies to Dr. Jung, who I'm sure would understand and forgive.

Western psychology, and particularly the work of Carl Jung, offers a basic working concept that inside each of us there lives many images, or archetypes. Archetypes can be collective or personal. Collective archetypes are powerful images filled with meaning that come from the society we live in or even the entire world population. The moon, the sun, gold, darkness, king, queen, are examples of universal archetypes. Our personal archetypes most likely have very specific faces or forms attached to them. Your mother, your father, the church you attended as a child, your first pet, your fifth grade teacher or the first flower a boy gave you might be examples of personal archetypes. These archetypes, or images, when you encounter them, fill you with very specific feelings associated with your relationship with the form of the thing or body of the person that created that feeling in you the first time, or many times in the early part of your life.

Remember our bus ride? Remember how we knew who all the passengers were and what they were like in their private lives? Well, we were projecting some archetypes onto them: Goddess, Evil Witch, Good Father, Cruel Barbarian (Bad Father?), Angelic Youth.

These archetypes or inner selves are usually the most important of our personal archetypes. These inner selves are actually part of our psychological makeup, which has been shaped by history, literature, religion, storytelling, and real people in our past, particularly our early childhood, when we are so impressionable. Each of these "people" carries certain feelings for us. In my own case, for example, there is a person inside me who constantly tells me that nothing I do is good enough, that everything is lacking in some way. He tells me I am stupid, that my biggest problem is that I "don't think." When something I do doesn't come out the way I had planned, he makes me feel worthless. I can practically hear him whispering into my ear, "Well, of course this didn't work. *You* did it. You can't do anything right. Never could, never will." And then I feel terrible about myself.

This inner person is my Bad Father, who unfortunately behaves exactly the way my biological father behaved toward me. All through my adolescence my weekly job was to mow the lawn. Every Saturday morning I got up and mowed the lawn, and every Saturday when I was finished, my father would come outside, get the lawn mower from the garage where I had just put it away, and without ever saying a word, mow the lawn again—the right way.

When I published my second book, I dedicated it to my father. I took him an advance copy. When he had finished leafing through it—including the dedication, which I pointed out to him—he tapped the book with his index finger, then pointed to the bookcase in the living room and said, "When you have enough of these to fill that bookcase, then you'll be a writer." Moments like that and the feelings that go along with them become deeply embedded in the psyche.

One of the things I did before leaving my last job was design and teach a seminar for some of the county's AIDS health service providers. It was well-received, and the next day my boss came into my office. "That was an excellent seminar you put on yesterday," he said. "Next time let's include the staff from our offices upstairs." I became immediately depressed. When he left my office I closed the door and was sick to my stomach.

Why? Why on earth would I have that response?

I realized much later—in therapy, I think—that I had that unreasonable response because it felt as though he said, "You could have done better if you had thought to include the staff from our offices upstairs. You should have thought of that. You would have thought of that if you weren't so stupid. Your problem is you don't think. When you have enough books to fill a book-case, then you'll get my respect. Then maybe I'll love you." It felt that way because I was projecting my Bad Father onto my boss. What he said stirred up the feelings I had the day my father denigrated my accomplishment in writing and publishing a book. It brought to the surface the feelings I had every Saturday morning of my adolescence as my father got out the lawn mower and made his devastating silent statement to me.

My boss became for me in that moment my Bad Father, and if I had remained unaware of it, I would have continued to see him in that light, in spite of the fact that he really liked my seminar. He even used the word "excellent," although I didn't hear it at the time. Not only did he like it, he wanted to offer it to the entire staff. But I was going on my feelings, not on what he said. Something inside got triggered, and I projected onto him a certain value: the value I place upon my father when he is abusing me. *It's never about what it's about!*

BACK TO OUR MAIN POINT

Keeping in mind our definition of "values" and the concepts of "projections of our own minds" as well as our inner selves, let's look at how we can manage them. Perhaps we can get them to behave better and not bully us. Wouldn't it be wonderful if we could take charge of our own psyches and thereby take charge of our own lives?

My particular inner selves include a Bad Father (my biological father), a Good Father (my uncle Bill), a Bad Mother (a combination of my biological mother and some other women in my life), a Good Mother (a combination of my aunt Cecilia, Mrs. Cohen—who helped raise me—and my biological mother), and then the most important of all: Krandy, the Child. Krandy is my personal archetype for the Child, but he comes in several forms. He can be my personal archetype for the Angelic Youth I was projecting onto the schoolboy back in the bus example a while ago. He can also be Krandy the Abandoned, the child who was left with the downstairs neighbor every day when his parents went off to work. Because I am an only child, he can be Krandy the Forgotten, a child lost in a sea of adults. Or he can be Krandy the Spoiled, pouting and sullen because he can't have his way. There are many Krandies, but they all have one thing in common: they are all innocent, tender, full of potential, and have enormous feelings which they don't understand.

Krandy the Abandoned is absolutely petrified of being left by the ones he loves because every day for the first six years of his life, while his mother went off to work he was left with Mrs. Cohen, who was elderly, overweight, strict, and not as much fun as his mother. Krandy is confused about his relationship to his father because his father slept all day and worked all night, and he practically never saw him. He is lonely because as an only child he had very few friends his own age. Krandy was around adults most of the time. He feels unloved because his mother was prone to violent mood swings, and his father never showed any affection to either him or his mother. Krandy's grandmother (his father's mother), who lived with them for many years, was a strict disciplinarian.

As a teenager, he was fat and ridiculed by nearly everyone in school, including many of the male teachers, which just reinforced his feelings toward men as being bad fathers. So Krandy holds lots of feelings right on the surface and is the most important and dear to me of all my inner selves. He is the sweet, loving, vulnerable, needy child who never asked for anything other than to be loved.

In the beginning I mentioned how common it is for people to say that pets are like our children. I believe that's true, but with a twist. I think pets are not "like" our children. I think they are *us* as children. I believe we project our inner child onto our pets and treat them accordingly, either the way we were treated as children—following the parental models given to us by our own parents—or the way we wanted to be treated as children but weren't.

When Hari is sick, why does it disturb me so deeply? For one thing, I love this animal very much. He is my best pal. I feel sad whenever anyone I love suffers. But the intensity of the pain I feel is a clear sign to me that something else is going on. I have projected Krandy onto Hari, and I respond to him as though I were responding to Krandy. Why do I make this projection? It's very simple to understand: Hari—like all dogs unless they have been terribly abused—is unconditionally loving, loyal, affectionate, and most of all, vulnerable. Just like I was when I was a child.

So on some unconscious level of my mind, when I take care of Hari I am taking care of Krandy the way Krandy wanted to be taken care of. I protect and defend him; I touch and pet him almost every time I am within arm's reach of him; I kiss and hug him; I even talk to him, telling him he's handsome and smart and what a good boy he is.

Am I only talking to Hari? I think not. I think I am talking to Krandy, who never heard those things from his father, who was rarely touched or hugged or kissed, except once in a while by aunts or his mother, and who seldom got praised for anything. I think I talk to him in the unconscious hope that it will somehow heal the wounds inside me.

Since coming to the awareness that Hari represents me as a child, I have begun talking to myself almost as much as I talk to Hari. I visualize or imagine myself as Krandy the 6-year-old and I tell him how sweet he is, how smart and lovable he is, and that I am never going to leave him. I tell him he can have all of his feelings, even the bad ones, and I'm neither going to try to take them away from him nor try to make him feel better (which would be just another form of trying to take them away from him). I tell him I'll be there with him while he feels sad or lonely; in fact, I'll feel those things along with him. When the feelings pass, we'll have some fun together.

Sometimes I talk to Krandy the 13-year-old, who was grossly overweight and extremely self-conscious. I tell him that I know he feels fat and ugly and as if he can't do anything right. I tell him I understand what it's like to be teased by his schoolmates and to hate sports. I tell him that I understand how lonely and unattractive he feels. And I also tell him that although he may not feel as if it's true, the fact is he will grow up to be a handsome, intelligent, wise, and extremely popular man. "I know that's hard to believe, and you don't feel as if that could ever really happen," I tell him, the way a good father might speak to a son, "but trust me on this one, because I know. I'm talking to you from the future, and I can assure you it will be all right in the end. Just hang in there. Even though it doesn't feel like it right now, you're doing just fine. I'm proud of you and I love you and I'll always be with you."

In other words, I say all the things to that "child" part of myself that my father never said to me, all the things I secretly wished my father would say, all the things a good father would say to his son. So once I realize I am projecting my inner child onto Hari, I can say to Krandy some of the things I've been saying to Hari.

When I think back to the time when my old dog Axel was so sick and having all those tests, I realize something very enlightening. Not only was I projecting Krandy's feelings onto Axel, but I was also projecting something else. I was projecting onto him my feelings about dying. I find myself doing the same thing now with Hari, whenever *he* gets sick.

As a person with AIDS there are many difficult things to face. Each illness, each infection, each day I am too tired to leave the house, these are all feelings I want to avoid. And I'm really good at it. I tell myself there's a flu going around, maybe I've got a touch of it; I remind myself that I stayed up late last night or went bike riding the day before or that I'm almost 50 years old, so why shouldn't I be tired sometimes? Anything but the virus. Anything but the terminal illness that is busy doing its work inside my body. Anything but facing the difficult truth.

So, getting back to my original story—when Axel became ill and was dribbling urine around the house, what did it mean to me? On some level I felt myself in the advanced stages of this illness, incontinent, ravaged by HIV and a host of opportunistic infections I can't do anything about. When Axel had to undergo test after test—blood tests, urine analyses, kidney biopsies—what went on inside me? It felt as if it were me undergoing those tests, waiting for the doctor to call and say things have gotten worse and I need to start a new treatment. When I worried that there might be something going on inside Axel's body that would mean I must put him to sleep, I felt my own ultimately incurable illness and my own eventual confrontation with the moment of death.

One might easily ask, "What's the point of all this awareness if it just makes you feel bad?" The point is, we must feel bad if we are to experience the fullness of human existence. Life is not just feeling good; it is a mixture of joy and sorrow. If I don't allow myself to "feel the pain," then how am I going to "feel the gain" of my experiences in life? I am, after all, a human being.

If I can raise my consciousness to a level where I am aware each time I am projecting something onto another person or situation, then maybe I can learn to "un-project" it, take it back into myself and deal with the real issue and not the external thing or person that triggered it. If I can "own it," as Californians love to say, then there is a better chance that I can deal with what's going on inside me. I can stop blaming the world for making me feel bad and realize that the world is simply filled with "triggers" or "buttons" that set off in me an entire array of emotional reactions that go deep down inside my mind and heart as well as way back into the history of my childhood, when Krandy was just an angelic youth trying to be loved by the people around him.

The secret to a happy life is knowing and, when possible, experiencing that everything begins and ends in me. As the great Viktor Frankl used to say, "I may not always be able to control the situation I am in, but I can always control my attitude toward it."

YES, PLEASE

I had an experience with my late partner Andre that taught me one of the most important lessons of my life: The importance of holding both joy and sorrow; the lesson of having a truly human experience in this life.

About three months before he died Andre was terribly sick with several opportunistic infections, including spinal meningitis. One night after having had a lumbar puncture, or "spinal tap," he was in an unimaginable ocean of pain. He was in the bedroom and I was in the living room reading this treatise by Schopenhauer— why, I haven't a clue; I guess I had read all of Danielle Steele's novels by that time. At any rate, I came across this brilliant passage, and I went in and lay down next to him and read it to him. He listened intently, which took every ounce of concentration he could muster. I can still see him as he struggled to turn over so he could face me and give me his full attention as I read. His face contorted, and he let out this little muffled cry, like a puppy when you frighten it or come close to stepping on its foot.

The passage went something like this: Why is it that a person walking down a street, seeing a speeding bus about to run over a man who is frozen in fear in the middle of the road, will, without thinking, without any concern for his own well-being, rush from the safety of the sidewalk and push that person out of harm's way, sometimes even sacrificing his own life for the stranger's? Why? Because somewhere deep inside, our hero knows that he and the person frozen in fear before the speeding bus are really one and the same. He knows that on some transcendent level they are really one person and one life and that in saving the other person's life he is actually saving his own.

Furthermore, if a person is going to fully and actively participate in the world as a human being, then he must say "Yes" to life, to all of life, the joys and the sorrows of human existence. He must accept all the world hands him, including the pain of sacrificing his life to save the life of another.

When I had finished reading it, I closed the book and smiled at him. I said, "Isn't that a brilliant insight?"

"No," Andre answered.

I was incredulous. That piece was so "Andre" that I was certain he would swoon over it. I also thought it would sort of inspire him to bear with his current dip into hell. I thought it might help him see the pain as a necessary part of his human experience on earth. The pain from the meningitis was bad enough, but the added pain of the lumbar puncture, where they stuck a needle the size of Wyoming into his spinal cord, had produced the most intolerable headaches. He couldn't bear even to blink his eyes. Yet he indulged me this reading and even engaged me in a bit of conversation.

"No?" I said.

He said, "It's not enough."

"What do you mean it's not enough?"

"You have to say 'Yes, please,'" Andre said softly.

I said, "I don't think I could ever get to that point. That's way too enlightened for me."

He said, "You will. You'll see."

I was sure he was wrong. But now—finally—I know differently. It's not enough to simply accept what comes along; we have to ask for all of it. Now, seeing the world through the eyes of AIDS, seeing the world and my life for what it really is, I feel differently. Remembering that image of Andre lying on his side, his eyes almost glazed over with the drugs he was on, is like an image of a reclining Buddha. And his words ring true to me. I see that he was right, that we must say "Yes, please" if we are going to have all of our life. If we're going to have a fully human experience, we must have joy and sorrow both. We must experience happiness and sadness, ecstasy and depression, and everything in between. Otherwise we've had some other sort of life, not human, but something else.

CONCLUSION

So when I trip over Hari, my challenge is to keep Hari distinct from all or any of my inner selves. I must find a way to know when my feelings about the present are being mixed up with feelings from the past. If my dog is sick, it is imperative for me to realize that Hari is the one having health problems and that I feel sad about it, but the dog is not me. Hari is a wonderful companion whom I love a great deal. My feelings about him are my feelings about him. If I have other feelings about me as a child or about me as a person with AIDS who is moving closer to the end of his life, I want those feelings to be as distinct and separate as possible. In other words, I want to be fully conscious of what is going on inside me. Only then can I have an appropriate response to life and direct that response in an appropriate manner.

When my boss is telling me my presentation was good and we should include more people next time, my challenge is to remember that my boss is my boss, not my father. When he says we should have more people next time, he's not saying I should have thought of having more people the first time; he's saying the presentation was better than he imagined it would be, and in fact it's so good he wants to share it with others.

When my doctor tells me I'm dying of AIDS I want to be able to see her as a human being doing her job and realize she can only keep me relatively healthy and comfortable for a while; she cannot keep me from dying. My doctor is a person who went to medical school and studied medicine; she is not the Almighty Healer, the Fountain of All Medical Knowledge, The Curer of All Illnesses. I must talk to her as a person, not cower from her as though she is a divine deity. I don't want to go around for the next year screaming at her, my partner, my coworkers, and my friends because I'm mad and scared that I'm dying. I want to talk to Krandy the Abandoned, who is scared, and to Krandy the Overweight Adolescent, who feels rejected and ugly and is angry about it. I want to find a way to express my fear, rage, and depression without acting out on the people around me who have nothing to do with my illness.

When people honk or recklessly cut in front of me in traffic or when a pedestrian flips me off, my challenge is not to hear my father telling me I don't have enough books on the shelf but to remember that this act isn't personal. These people will go through their entire day honking at dozens of others, pulling in front of many cars, giving the finger to lots of other people, and when they get home they'll yell at the people they live with for no apparent reason. For in their lives, as in mine, it's never about what it's about. Who knows what terrible baggage they're carrying around and what their inner selves really look like? Who knows what triggered their projections onto me and caused such acting out? My job is to make sure I don't do the same thing.

When I feel nervous or anxious or sad or threatened or depressed, my challenge is to make room for those feelings because they are part of the human experience. If I can remember where the feelings come from and how to talk to the parts of me (my inner selves) who carry those feelings, I can manage them without them managing me.

CHAPTER FOUR

ACTING CRAZY, STAYING SANE: WHAT WE CAN DO TO CHANGE THINGS

Nothing makes me angrier than a person telling me what's wrong but never offering any suggestions as to how I might fix it. Once we can at least identify where the feelings are coming from—what it's really about—there are some simple tools and practical skills we can use to help ourselves begin to change.

A PERSONAL STORY

I sought out a therapist in 1987 when my best friend was dying of AIDS and my life partner Andre and I had both been diagnosed HIV positive. It felt as if the world was caving in on me and I was going to be left alone, my most terrifying fear. One of the most important points in my development occurred around a dream I had about a month after I began my therapy. The dream went like this:

I am driving a sports car near Calistoga, California, where I grew up. I stop at a country store to buy some food. Inside is an empty room with a fireplace. At one end of the room is a frosted glass wall with a door, also of frosted glass. To my left is a beaded curtain covering a doorway to another room, and to my right is a fireplace. A woman dressed like a gypsy comes through the beaded curtain, carrying a baby about one or two years old. I ask for a sandwich, and she sets the baby on the very narrow mantel above the fireplace and goes back through the beaded curtain without saying a word.

The baby is teetering and about to fall, so I grab him and hold him. The gypsy woman returns with a man I presume to be her husband. She begins to berate me and tell me she doesn't sell things to people like me. Then her husband begins to berate me as well. Behind the glass door, I can make out the figure of a beautiful man taking a shower. Standing perfectly still in front of the glass wall watching all this is a beautiful young woman. The gypsy couple grab the baby out of my arms and shoo me out of the store, shouting epithets at me and saying they don't allow people like me in their store. Now we are outside and I am getting into my car. The couple is shouting from the steps. The other couple—the man from the shower and the beautiful woman—are standing silently beside the gypsy couple, watching me as I get in the car and drive away. I recognize the store as a store I used to see when my parents and I would drive up to my uncle Wes' ranch. I turn up the road toward my uncle's house and speed away.

The morning after this dream I woke up remembering every vivid detail and feeling quite disturbed. It was a Saturday, the morning I used to take my dog out to Golden Gate Park, so I loaded him into the car and off we went. I couldn't get the dream out of my mind, especially the feeling of holding the baby while its parents shouted at me. I asked myself over and over what it meant. I remembered my therapist telling me that every character in my dreams is an aspect of me (one of my inner selves, a facet of my own personality). So I went through my dream characters one by one and began to realize who they were.

THE INNER SELVES

The gypsy woman was my Bad Mother, the feminine energy in my life that turns moody and morose unexpectedly, like my mother did, screaming wildly and throwing things, denigrating me for the slightest infraction or for no rational reason at all.

The husband in the dream, who assisted the gypsy woman in running me out of the store, was the Bad Father who lives in me, who, like my father, was never visible unless conjured up and cajoled by my mother in one of her moods. He would then take my mother's side in any matter just to appease her and keep her from turning her wrath on him.

The man behind the shower door was my Good Father, and the woman standing at the end of the room was my Good Mother. Like my Uncle Bill and Aunt Jenny—who lived far away with their happy family, out of my reach and therefore unable to protect me—both of these people in the dream were beautiful, both of them silent, both of them useless to me in a crisis. They stood by and watched as the bad parents abused me.

And, of course, there was the most important figure of all, the baby: me, the inner child, abused, not cared for, toted around like a thing rather than a person, left to fend for himself in the most precarious of situations—like being placed on a narrow mantel— and treated with complete lack of consciousness.

In the dream I took the child into my own arms. I kept the

child from falling, from suffering the effects of the callous Bad Mother's and Bad Father's lack of concern. Since no one in the dream was going to protect this innocent infant, I stepped up and took him into my arms.

As I walked through Golden Gate Park, the dog bounding around through the bushes, bringing me sticks and pine cones to throw for him, I realized that I must protect that inner child in just the way I would protect my dog. I must love him the same way I love my dog. Then in a spontaneous moment of complete individuation, a moment of courage and rebellion, I called forth each of the characters in my dream, imagined them standing before me, and spoke to them.

To the gypsy woman, the Bad Mother, I said, "You may never abuse this child again. I am taking him from you to keep by my side for the rest of his life. You will never again put him in a dangerous or hurtful situation."

To the Bad Father, her husband, I said, "You may never shout at me like that again. You may speak to me at any time, saying anything you like in a civilized way, but you will never again be permitted to yell abusive insults at me. Never."

To the Good Mother and Good Father I said, "And you two, beautiful as you are, tender and gentle as you are, you are of no use to me if you don't step forward and protect me. If you won't speak up for me, you are as bad as the other two. From now on you must help me; you must show your love for me by standing up for me in difficult times. You must encourage and support me, make me feel strong and capable."

I imagined the child cradled in my arms. I actually folded my arms as though I were holding a baby—we were deep in the woods by now, so I was alone and there was no one passing by who would think I had lost my mind (although by this time I couldn't have cared less). To him I very gently said, "You will never be hurt again so long as you live. I will keep you with me always and protect you and love you and be with you whenever you need me."

Then, imagining them all walking alongside me down the trail through the woods, I said, "Each of you is a part of me. Each of you lives inside me. And as difficult as it is sometimes, I welcome and honor you all. There must be room inside me for all of you, since you make up who I am. But understand this and make no mistake about it: While I will make room for you and I will always listen to what you have to say—as though I could shut you up— none of you will ever be allowed to gain control of me again. None of you can abuse me; none of you can throw tantrums; none of you can hurt me by your action or inaction. I will honor you and your thoughts and feelings by listening to them. You must honor me by submitting to my authority. I am in charge here, and my first priority is to protect and defend and love this child, who holds the most tender and most fragile of all my feelings. You must all submit to my authority to manage you and keep you balanced. That is how it will be from this moment on. I am the boss."

That was a turning point in my life. From that morning on, whenever I was having strong emotional reactions to things, feelings I felt I could hardly control, I called my inner selves forward and talked to them one by one until I found the one who was acting up. Then I would talk to that part of myself as a loving, good father or a close friend might, telling him or her that I heard what he or she was saying and I would take it into consideration, but there could be no mutiny allowed, no acting out, no berating the child, no hurting me anymore.

Although I could not have put it in mythological or spiritual terms at the time, I think this was when my ego began working in service of the Self.

PROTECTING THE SOUL

There is a marvelous story in India that the Hindus tell about the origin of one of their most important gods, Ganapati, or Ganesha, Remover of Obstacles. The god Shiva was married to the goddess Parvati. They were very much in love and had an ideal relationship except for one thing. Every once in a while Shiva would go off hunting in the Himalayas and not come home for nine or ten thousand years.

Because Parvati was such an extraordinary beauty many men in the city where they lived would pester her after Shiva had been gone for awhile. They would come to the palace and visit her at court telling her she should dump that no-good husband of hers. "If he really cared about you he wouldn't go off hunting for so long," they would say. Each, in turn, would propose marriage to her. And she, in turn, would brush them off. But it just got worse and worse as time went by.

Finally, men were finding out when she took her bath and would come sneaking into her chamber just to get a glimpse of her wondrously beautiful body. Parvati had enough of this, and one day she scraped her arms with a coarse brush, took the dry skin that came off, and out of this skin made herself a son.

He was beautiful, like his mother, and strong and brave, like his father. He was born fully grown and powerful, and she told him, "I want you to stand outside my bath every day and let no one enter, no matter who they are or what they tell you. These men are horrible. They won't leave me alone, yet they know I am committed only to your father, Shiva. Stop anyone who would enter here, no matter what you must do."

"I will keep all intruders out, Divine Mother. Have no fear at all. I shall remove all obstacles to your taking your bath in peace." And so her son stood outside her bath. He wore a magnificent tunic, and at his side hung a golden sword.

By and by, Shiva returned from his hunting trip and went looking for Parvati. Her maidservants told him that she was in the royal bath, so he made straight for her chambers to tell her he was home and wanted to make love with her. He couldn't wait to see her. After all, ten thousand years is a long time to be away from the one you love. When he arrived at the entrance to the royal bath, he encountered the young man at the door. "Halt," the young man said. "You cannot enter here. Go away."

"Out of my way, runt," Shiva exclaimed and started to push the boy aside. The young man drew his sword and challenged Shiva, saying, "No one may enter the royal bath. Parvati is quietly bathing and is indisposed. You must leave or face your own death."

"Ha!" cried Shiva and drew his own weapon, "You obviously don't know with whom you're dealing. You shall be the one to die." Before the young man could respond, Shiva had sliced off the boy's head and flung it out the window with such force it flew all the way to Lanka, a thousand miles away. Hearing the scuffle, Parvati came running out. Seeing her son lying on the floor headless, she began to scream and weep inconsolably.

"Our son, our son," she wailed. "That was our son you have killed." Shiva, seeing his wife's pain and now feeling dreadful, looked around and saw an elephant walking by outside. He ran out, cut off the elephant's head, and placed it on his son, restoring his life.

This is how Ganesha, the elephant-headed god, was created and how he came to be known as the Remover of Obstacles. He is worshipped throughout India and is probably the most popular deity in the country. No endeavor, however small, is undertaken by a Hindu without a small prayer to Ganesha to remove the obstacles in the devotee's path. (Interestingly, Ganesha is also the one who places obstacles into the path of his devotees when it will be beneficial for them.)

When I heard this myth it struck a deep chord in me. I saw in it a metaphor of my own psyche and my inner selves. I think of Parvati as the soul, the inner feminine aspect of the human psyche. She is where all nurturing, all caring, all loving resides. She is the creative, affectionate energy that protects and nourishes. She needs time alone, time to contemplate and rejuvenate herself.

I see Shiva as pure masculine energy. It is the assertive energy of action that gets things accomplished, but often at the expense of the soul. I am often tempted to think of this kind of pure power as energy without consciousness. In order for the soul to be protected, there must be a merger of the two. There must be some hybrid product of masculine and feminine energy to strike a balance; thus, Ganesha is born. What better figure to symbolize the union of yin and yang, of feminine and masculine energies, than the elephant? The elephant is quiet, contemplative, slow and deliberative, almost thoughtful (yin). Yet the elephant is the most powerful force in the jungle, able to crush virtually anything that stands in its way (yang).

It is Ganesha who will remove the obstacles to the soul's peace and tranquillity. He will keep distractions away from her so she may rejuvenate herself and enjoy some contemplative time, where she can bring thought and feeling together. Ganesha, the elephant-headed god, is for me a metaphor for the enlightened ego, which goes before the soul (the Self) and removes obstacles in its path, like the elephant in India walking before the members of a wedding ceremony, trampling down the jungle in its path, removing all obstacles to their progression. It often reminds me of the biblical passage "Make straight the way of the Lord." Parvati is "the Lord" of the soul, that part of us which is God Itself.

WHAT WE CAN DO

When I am conscious enough to realize one of my inner selves is gaining the upper hand (Bad Father, Bad Mother, Frightened Child, or whoever it is) and I call that aspect of myself forth and calm it down, I am, in effect, acting like Ganesha. My enlightened ego is managing my many inner selves so that the Self will not be damaged. I am making certain that the innocent child is not going to be hurt by some thoughtless aspect of myself.

Now it may seem extreme to some people to actually talk to yourself, but we do lots of silly things these days and think nothing of it. We dye our hair blue, pierce our eyebrows, spend a thousand dollars in Las Vegas in two days, run up credit card bills way beyond our ability to pay, have affairs with married people. What's a little talking to one's self in light of all that?

Paul has another way of managing his inner selves: He writes letters to them. He sits down and writes letters that are sometimes short and to the point, other times long and detailed, telling his inner selves that certain behavior has to stop. He will not tolerate any more acting out, any further belittling of him. For him, it's quite an effective tool.

I have yet another friend who, finding himself having a difficult day, will go to the nearest phone booth, pick up the receiver and imagine he is talking to his inner selves on the other end of the phone line. He will deliver his message, then go on his way. Sometimes he calls his soul, if he can't figure out which one of his inner selves is acting up. He will call his soul and tell her to hang on until he gets home and then he'll figure out what's wrong and start fixing it.

When I find that one of my inner selves has been running rampant and I have been acting out, I've stopped asking myself, "Why am I doing this?" I find it is more helpful to ask "What part of me is doing this?" This approach, I've found, makes it easier for the adult ego—the me who is asking the question—not to get defensive about taking ownership for the acting out or the uncomfortable feelings. It also gives that conscious part of me which is the adult ego some distance from the situation and allows it to summon up the enlightened ego as a mediator. If I ask the question "Why am I doing this?" very often I will become immediately defensive and start looking for excuses for the behavior or feelings rather than search for the reasons for them. That is simply human nature.

It doesn't matter what technique one uses as long as one finds some way to address the various aspects of the psyche when the need arises. By calling up the enlightened ego, the "manager of the inner selves," and articulating what will and will not be tolerated, you can calm some extremely troubled waters.

Once in a while, I can't locate the inner culprit. No matter how hard I try, I simply can't figure out where the disturbance is coming from. When that happens, I take the child into my arms or take him by the hand and say, sometimes aloud, "Try not to worry. It's going to be all right. I'm right here and I'm not going anywhere." This always has an immediate calming effect on me. If we can't fix the problem right away, we can at least put ourselves at rest. One of my most effective techniques, if I'm in the car, is to open my arms and say, "Come sit on my lap and you can steer." Then I visualize myself as a 6-year-old boy climbing onto my lap and taking hold of the wheel. This always makes me break into a smile because it was my favorite thing to do as a small boy and one of only a handful of happy memories I have with my father. I would suggest that approach for anyone in a time of emotional crisis. Think of something you used to do as a child that made you feel really happy and safe; then imagine you are doing that with yourself as a child. You are the adult, and the child is right there next to you.

The reason I suggest visualizing or fantasizing yourself as a child and addressing that part of you is because it seems it is most often the child who carries the fragile feelings and always the child who panics. It is the child who feels overwhelmed and confused by the actions of others (Bad Father, Bad Mother) and always blames him/herself. By speaking to the frightened child, the enlightened ego can be quite comforting and reassuring. After all, isn't that all any of us really want in the long run? Someone next to us when it gets dark?

Paul's and my personal experience in this comes primarily from sitting at deathbed after deathbed, speaking words of comfort and reassurance, love and encouragement to people who are actively dying. They are frightened, unsure, and most of all, do not want to go alone into that dark, mysterious void. Like the

Good Mother or Good Father, like the enlightened ego, we would speak soft, loving, and comforting words to them. We would try to let them know that in some sense they were not going alone and that we would stay right there with them until the crossing was complete. There is great comfort in simply not being alone in a traumatic situation. By learning to become your own enlightened ego and giving it a voice, you perform that service for the most important person in your life: you.

CHAPTER FIVE

LIFE IS BUT A DREAM (SHABOOM, SHABOOM)

One of the most insightful things Paul has ever said to me he said one day as we were walking up Castro Street in our San Francisco neighborhood. We came out of our local bookstore and had to walk around two people who were shouting at each other. They were arguing over something one of them was holding. We couldn't tell what it was, and we understood that it didn't really matter, since it's never about what it's about. They were each claiming ownership of it and listing all the reasons the other person should give up all claims to it. As we walked around them, Paul shook his head sadly and took my hand. "People just don't see the poetry of life, do they?"

"Say more," I said, which is what I always say when I don't understand his meaning.

"They don't see the metaphors. If only we could look at each day as a dream, then maybe we'd understand what it was all about." It was truly one of the most profound and useful insights into human behavior I have ever heard. We have worked with it ever since.

Looking at life's "outer world" as metaphorical is like looking at life the same way we'd look at our dreams. By interpreting our life the way we would interpret a dream we gain intriguing and helpful insights into how our inner selves may be influencing us throughout the day. As we project our inner selves onto the outer world we react to the world the way we react to those parts of our selves. We do this in dreams all the time and understand it metaphorically. But we also do it during waking hours when our inner selves flare up and start taking control of our feelings.

Over and above that, if we look at each encounter as a dream, we might see how the universe is speaking to us in symbols and metaphors. If the world is a projection of our own minds on any level, then each image we take in during the day deserves to be looked at on all levels. For example, even the scene of those two people arguing in front of the bookstore deserves to be looked at to see what message or lesson was present in it for me. Who were those two people? Why did I encounter them? What part of me did they represent? Why did I react to them the way I did?

Each evening, if we sit and review our day, think back over what we did, the people we encountered and what our reactions were, we might gain more insight if we interpret those events and those people as dream events and dream characters.

TRUTH AND FACT

In the marvelous book *Black Elk Speaks*, Black Elk, an ancient Native American holy man of the Oglala Sioux tribe, tells many stories. They are a compilation of visions he had during the span of his life. They are also the myths of his people, which are sacred to him and his Sioux nation. After telling one of the most powerful of the visions, that of the White Bison Woman, Black Elk speaks these words of wisdom: "This they tell, and whether it happened so or not, I do not know; but if you think about it, you can see that it is true."

All holy men, shamans, prophets, sages, and artists in every genre know that the words Black Elk speaks are of the deepest kind of wisdom. What is important is what takes place in the inner world—not what the facts are, but what the truth is.

Two years ago a friend of ours came into some money and purchased a beautiful home on seven acres of redwoods along the coast. She and her partner were planning to use it as a summer hideaway. When she and her partner took possession of the property they invited us to visit them the first weekend they spent in the house. They also asked if we would devise some sort of ritual to mark the occasion.

That weekend we drove up and joined our two friends the day before they were to return to the city. We had a leisurely lunch on the deck, and then the four of us enacted an hourlong ritual of consecrating the land and marking the passage from one caretaker to another. The next day, just before they left, they called us into the kitchen and presented us with a key to the house, saying, "Consider this place yours. Come as often as you like. Write here, rest here, replenish yourselves here." Needless to say, we were quite flabbergasted and moved to tears.

If I look at that day as though it were a dream, I might see it this way:

I go into the woods, where there is an abundance of life (trees, bushes, birds, animals), and where I can look out over the ocean (the unconscious). I am among living, growing, vibrant things, but very near my inner self (the ocean, the unconscious). While I am there, my Anima, or inner feminine (my woman friend who bought the house), along with my counterpart, or alter ego (Paul), and his anima (my friend's partner) perform a ritual that consecrates the land (nature, the source of life) and the house (my complex inner world) which rests upon it. The four of us walk through each room of the house (each area of my personality) ringing bells (awakening consciousness) and waving incense (an act of worship and valuing). This ritual honors all the aspects of who I am. We do the same outside, around the property, paying honor to all the growing, living things that abound in this fertile place (creativity and creation). The ritual (act of praise and thanksgiving) is led by me (ego) and Paul (my projected soul/Self) and has been created by us together (ego and Self).

The message seems to be that this is the "right" way for me to be functioning. In the "dream" I am engaging in spiritual practice and allowing my soul expression through my writing (the creation of the ritual of consecration). As a reward for this "right action," Anima presents me with the "key" to my personality or major "complex" (the house) and tells me to visit this consecrated place often, to write there, to rest and replenish my soul there. This is a place of rejuvenation, a "soul" place where I can be in touch with the divine in me through my writing. This is a place and an activity that will always be rewarded, but only if I honor it, acknowledge that it is sacred, and respect it.

Sounds pretty accurate to me. This sounds exactly like the way in which I try to live my life, the way my heart and soul tell me to live it. When I told Paul my interpretation of our weekend with our friends, he reminded me that two years previous to our visit, we had spent a week in a place not far from our friend's property called Sea Ranch. This is a planned community of million-dollar homes in a very tightly controlled, gated community overlooking the ocean along the Pacific Coast Highway. We were quite uncomfortable there since there were so many rules about where to park, where you could have your dog, what to do with your garbage, etc. We felt as if we were in a fascist country.

One day while we were walking along the beach Paul said, "I wouldn't mind living up here in the woods, but I'd want to have a house up there." He was pointing to the hills on the other side of the highway, overlooking the ocean. He was pointing to the hilltop where our friends' future house was standing. Now, two years later, his wish came true. As I thought of our weekend as though it were a dream to interpret, I couldn't help but think of the line from the old song "A dream is a wish your heart makes."

HEAVEN'S GATE

Over a three-day period toward the end of March 1997, 39 people who were part of a religious cult called "Heaven's Gate" performed a ritual mass suicide in Rancho Santa Fe, California. The entire country was shocked. The news spread throughout the world, and within hours hundreds of reporters were storming the neighborhood where it happened.

The members of Heaven's Gate were men and women ranging in age from their mid 20s to their early 70s. They supported themselves by designing Web sites for the Internet. The president of the company they worked for said they were friendly, intelligent, hardworking people. He never had any reason to complain about them or their work and was startled when he came upon the scene at the house where they carried out their suicides.

For about a month prior to the event, a comet known as the Hale-Bopp comet had been visible in the sky and would continue being visible for another several weeks. The cult's leader, who went by the name of Do (as in Do-Re-Mi), told his followers there was a spaceship following the comet. The spaceship was hiding in the comet's wake so it couldn't be detected by anyone on earth. Do told his followers that the spaceship had come to take them to the heavenly kingdom. They would all have to prepare themselves and join him in drinking a lethal mixture of alcohol and barbiturates.

As the group prepared for their death ritual they made a videotape. Two by two, they appeared on the tape and said good-bye to people. They each wanted people to know how happy they were and that they were doing this out of their deep religious beliefs. They said they had not been brainwashed, and they were excited and happy about what was going to happen. They wished everyone could understand what they were about to do and be as happy as they were.

They did appear to be extremely happy. They were laughing, smiling, and giggling. The excited, childlike anticipation on their faces and in their demeanor was readily apparent. Most striking to me was the speech of a young man, perhaps just 20 years old. He looked like many of the young men in our neighborhood: crew cut hairdo, handsome, carefree, filled with the vigor of youth. He was so excited, so animated. So ready to go to heaven.

The media was ghoulish in their coverage. For two days in Southern California (and perhaps in most of the rest of the country), the television coverage went on virtually 24 hours a day. Day and night helicopters circled the house where the suicides took place, the video cameras aboard zooming down for close-ups of the coroner's staff carrying the bodies out of the mansion on stretchers, one by one, all 39 of them.

Reporters and photographers waited at the coroner's office to film the bodies being unloaded from the large refrigerator trucks that had to be brought in to accommodate so many corpses in the little town of Rancho Santa Fe. As the days went on and autopsies were conducted, it was discovered that several of the men, including the cult leader, had been castrated. None of them had any record of family, and no family members contacted the sheriff's office for days. All of the cult members had ceased all contact with the people and places they had come from.

Over the next week, television news broadcasts, talk shows, radio programs, and people in the streets all over the country were talking about this mass suicide. And what were they saying? Everyone was saying the same thing, using the same language: tragic, crazy, pathetic, brainwashed, insane, mad, victimized. I soon began to realize that Paul and I were the only ones who were seeing any of this a bit differently. While we were saddened and shocked at the event, we were also seeing the "poetry" of it.

I began asking people questions, a bit rhetorically, I admit. The reactions I got quickly convinced me I must stop asking these questions, at least out loud.

THE INNER JOURNEY, OUTER SIGNS, AND RITUALS

Every religious belief system tells us the spiritual journey is an inner journey. It doesn't take place in the outer world; there is not a city of Baptism or a Bris County; we do not move at the age of 12 to the town of Confirmation or Bar Mitzvah. It sounds silly even to say such things.

There are no physical places in our minds, only spiritual, emotional, or mental states of mind; they are not states like Colorado or New Hampshire. But the signs and rituals we use to mark our progress on this inner journey are on the outside. They do exist in the material world. We engage in rites such as marriage, last rites, and ordination to make more concretely apparent to us things that are taking place on the inside, in the inner world. We place a ring on someone's hand. The ring is not the marriage; it is a symbol of the marriage. We carve or paint a six-pointed star on the building where we worship, not because the star is our religious belief but because it is a symbol of our religious belief.

These symbols are important to us, and our rituals are rites of passage that we would never give up. They are signposts on the road of our spiritual journey. We believe in ritual, and enacting them somehow transforms us in our inner world, even though the rituals themselves are conducted in the outer world. (These are, of course, the very things we fight with one another about. These symbols have become emblems of war. We have killed one another for centuries because we disagree about which symbols and rituals are the "right" ones. But that's for a later chapter.)

So I began to ask myself—and others around me—some questions about the cult known as Heaven's Gate.

- Did anyone who watched the videotape the cult members left behind notice how happy all those people were? Did anyone see the joy in their faces?

- Didn't Christ also say to abandon family, leave father and mother, and follow Him?

- If the spiritual journey is an inner journey and signs in the outer world are only markers of our progress on that journey, what's the difference between a comet over Rancho Santa Fe and a star over Bethlehem?

- If a ritual is an outer enactment of an inner commitment, how does the act of castration differ from the act of circumcision?

- If Christ were alive today and preaching that we should love Saddam Hussein and give all we have to the people of Iraq, would we detain Him for psychiatric evaluation?

- If someone reported there was a man in the local church smashing statues and turning over altars made of ivory and marble (the way Christ did in the temple), would we not arrest him?

- If there was a man sitting under a tree for seven years, like the Buddha did, wouldn't we petition a judge for a psychiatric examination?

- How is saying that a man died, got up three days later, and ascended into heaven any more preposterous than a man saying he is going to die and then be taken up in a spaceship (or a fiery chariot) that God is sending to take him to heaven?

THE POETRY OF LIFE

By looking at our lives in the same way we look at religion, dreams, or even a poem, we might come to quite a different understanding of who we are, what we're doing, and why we're doing it. If I realize that every person I encounter during my day is in some way related to my inner selves and is in some fashion just a reflection of some part of my own psyche, I might see people quite differently.

When I am knocked off my feet by a child running amok in the grocery store, instead of seeing someone else's undisciplined brat, I might see him as the 6-year-old child I once was, and I may understand my reaction to him better. I may even change my reaction to him—and to his parents.

If I see a dog running wild in the street, dodging cars, and instinctively chasing cats and squirrels, I might not see it as chaos or someone's pet out of control; I may be able to see it as a symbol of the unbridled life force exerting itself un–self-consciously—a force that excites, attracts, and frightens me all at the same time.

If I am moved either to tears or to trembling by the sight of a hunched-over old woman trying to climb the steps of her row house, perhaps I will see not just a stranger in the last days of her life but that part of me that feels old and tired or that part of me that is scared of death. And perhaps that will enable me to approach that part of myself and begin to feel differently.

No matter how we look at either dreams or our waking hours, there is more to see than meets the eye. Perhaps the only way we can ever truly understand the world around us is to see it the same way many Christians see Christ: not only as a man, but as a man and something else. Perhaps the only way we can ever truly understand the world around us is to see it as the ancients of the Orient and the poets and artists of all time have seen it: as a dream.

CHAPTER SIX

DIANA: A MODERN MYTH

Contemporary wise men Joseph Campbell and Robert A. Johnson have shown us quite clearly how the correct reading of myths can enlighten us on the human condition. Myths are a clear and direct way, albeit dressed in the costume of "story," to enter the inner world. Johnson has pointed out how whenever we encounter a myth or a play or any story of substance that speaks of a kingdom, we would do well to consider it a metaphor for the "inner kingdom" that is our own individual or collective psyche. We have in our midst a modern myth that has unfolded before us.

Like most myths, we have not been able to "read" the metaphors and unravel the symbolic meanings, partly because we are so caught up in the story itself, partly because when one is in the middle of a situation it is extremely difficult to gain any distance from it in order to understand it better. But the fable-like events of the British royal family during the past 20 years have provided us with a rare opportunity to do some substantial individual and collective introspection and some very important inner work.

When the Princess of Wales was killed in an automobile accident in September 1997, the entire world mourned. The world mourned as it never had in modern times. All around the globe people were completely disconsolate. In Great Britain, royal subjects traveled from every corner of the kingdom to be present at Princess Diana's funeral. They knew they wouldn't be allowed inside Westminster Abbey; they understood there was a good chance they might not even see the casket being taken to the church. Nevertheless, they came by the millions simply to keep vigil outside the great cathedral or stand along the route of the funeral procession.

They stood silently, holding bouquets of flowers, laying them at the gate of Kensington Palace, strewing them in the path of the hearse as it passed by. It seemed the entire kingdom was present, standing in utter silence along the entire 70-mile route as Princess Diana's body was borne to her final resting place. Why? Why did the world react with such intensity? Many other good and beautiful people have died tragic, untimely deaths. Princess Grace of Monaco, Marilyn Monroe, and countless others have met similar fates. What made this one so extraordinary in the individual and collective heart? This was the question everyone was asking.

The press reported on the accident for weeks afterward, trying to come to grips with the sudden death of someone so dearly loved by the entire world. Psychologists, counselors, columnists, pundits of every sort offered their opinions: She was someone who spoke to the people; she loved children; she was down to earth; she was beautiful; she helped the downtrodden; she symbolized the "outsider." On and on they waxed eloquent, these professional analysts of the modern age. Yet no one spoke of the inner world. No one said, "We are devastated because it's never about what it's about. We are devastated because Diana is us."

In his monumentally important work *The Fisher King and the Handless Maiden*, Robert A. Johnson details an ancient myth. I will summarize it here only for our purposes and try to do it justice, although I would urge every reader to find this book and read it in its entirety for a much more in-depth look at the subject.

There is a miller who lives in a mill and grinds grain into flour. He is married and has a young daughter. His method of grinding the grain is primitive and wears him out. One day the devil appears in disguise and tells the miller that he will show him how to make his work much easier, produce more flour, and become rich and live a leisured life. All the devil wants is what the miller has behind his house. The miller thinks for a moment and realizes that the only thing that stands behind his house is an old oak tree. He thinks this is more than fair and so agrees to the bargain.

The devil shows the miller how to harness the waters of the stream that runs alongside the mill and to use it to turn a stone and grind the grain into flour. Soon the miller is producing ten times the amount of flour and is wealthy beyond his wildest imaginings. But, of course, the devil returns one day to claim his price. He tells the miller to meet him out back. The miller goes to the back of the house, and standing there next to the oak tree is his young daughter. The miller is distraught, but nevertheless agrees to keep his bargain. He hands over his daughter to the devil with no protest whatsoever from his wife, and the devil chops off the daughter's hands. He then disappears.

Naturally, the daughter is horrified. The miller and his wife, however, proceed to tell the daughter that it's all right. She doesn't really need her hands any more. After all, they are rich and have servants to wait on the daughter's every need. And so life goes on in their household as before, except, of course, that the daughter, the handless maiden, is desperately sad and depressed. She can do nothing for herself. Every time she wants the least thing she must summon one of the servants to do it for her. If she complains, her father reminds her of the wonderful riches and prestige the new method of grinding grain into flour has brought into their lives. She is desolate, alone, estranged from all around her, and her parents either do not care or do not understand her plight—or perhaps both. As one might expect, our handless maiden runs away.

She flees into the forest and there she lives on the fruit from an orchard she discovers. She finds that if she stands on her tiptoes, she can eat the fruit from the lower branches, and this is how she keeps herself alive. What she doesn't know is that the orchard belongs to the king. The king learns of the beautiful maiden with no hands and goes to see for himself. Instantly, he falls in love with her and marries her. He takes her to his castle, where the first thing he does, along with making her pregnant, is order the royal silversmiths to cast silver hands for his new queen.

So now the handless maiden has two exquisite silver hands. They are, of course, quite useless, and her ignominy and pain are worse than before. Now she has hands that are beautiful but of no value. She possesses form but no function. She can neither feed her baby nor tend to her own simple needs. She must rely completely upon the servants at court. No matter what she says to her devoted husband who does truly love her, his answer is always the same: You don't need hands; you have servants to do your bidding. Naturally, she becomes despondent once again. She takes her baby and flees once more into the forest.

She isn't there long when a terrible thing happens. Her baby falls into the river and is drowning. She calls out instinctively for her servants, but, of course, there are no servants to hear her. Seeing her child drowning before her eyes, she does the only thing she can do. From the depths of her heart and soul, in spite of their uselessness, she reaches her silver hands into the river and scoops up her child. When she does this the child is saved, and, miraculously, her hands are restored to their normal state.

INTERPRETING THE MYTH

Johnson interprets for us how the myth, like all good myths and dreams, not only shows us the dilemma, but also presents us with the solution. The handless maiden is a metaphor for the feeling function in the modern world. The most tender feelings we have, represented here by a young maiden, are cast aside in favor of technology. With her mother's approval, her father makes a bargain with the devil to achieve progress and gain wealth, status, and self-aggrandizement. The sensitive young daughter—like our own inner feeling function—is pushed aside when she stands in the way of material gain.

How many times have we told ourselves to not talk back to the boss because it might affect our advancement at our jobs? How many times have we given up a weekend in the country in order to work overtime on a project at the office? When we set aside our visit to the gym, our lunch with a friend, even an hour's reading of a good book in order to tend to our "worldly" needs, we are chopping off the hands of that tender young part of our psyche that experiences the world through feeling. We are wounding our feeling function. We are telling ourselves that we don't deserve to relax, we don't need to feel the ocean's breeze on our face or to be thrilled by a character in a novel. In other words, we are saying that we don't need to have those experiences that emanate from the heart and soul. We decide it is acceptable to put them aside if they conflict with an opportunity to further our material gain in some way. Chop, chop, chop.

We tell ourselves that there will be time later to walk on the beach or that it's not really that important to go to the gym today. We tell our feeling function, that handless maiden part of our psyche that carries these delicate and tender sensibilities, that there's really no reason to indulge in feelings. We tell her that "we have servants for that." And who are those servants? Are they the movie stars we project our innermost feelings onto? Are they our wives and mothers and daughters? And what part of our inner self do they represent? What part of our inner self is paying the price for not going to the beach, not speaking up when we are angry, not curling up for an intimate evening of Agatha Christie or Robert Frost? Eventually, the "maiden" has little choice but to run away, or worse, become catatonic—that is, we lose our ability to feel anything.

We surround ourselves with these modern "mills," conveniences that make our physical life easier. We think absolutely nothing of chopping off our feeling function at every turn. Why, we even think it is more important to interrupt one telephone call with another rather than possibly miss out on some opportunity for new information, and so we install "call waiting," as though the feelings of the person we're talking to, not to mention our own inner feelings, are not worth considering. The feeling function in the modern world seems to have not only its hands chopped off but its feet as well. It feels, sometimes, as if we are hacking away at our very limbs. "The hell with feeling anything," we cry. "Find a way to put more random access memory onto a smaller microchip. Now there's something we can take to the bank!" Chop, chop, chop!

A MODERN TALE

Now let's look at the story of Princess Diana as though it were a modern myth. Let's look at it the way we might look at a dream from the inner world, trying to tell us something about our conscious stance in the outer world. Let me tell it like a fairy tale.

Once there was a beautiful maiden. She was tall, willowy, and graceful, and her beautiful, long golden hair was bright like the sun. Her father made an arrangement with the royal family that his daughter would marry the prince and become the princess of the land. One day she would be queen! That would certainly serve her family well in the future.

The palace held a press conference to announce the engagement, and reporters asked the couple all sorts of questions. One of the questions was how they felt about each other. The prince said he respected his fiancée and was impressed by the many wonderful attributes she possessed, including her amazing beauty. The princess was too shy to say much of anything at all. After they listed the qualities of their relationship there was one quality they forgot to mention, and so the reporter added it for them, in the form of a question. The reporter asked, "And love?" The princess blushed and said softly, "Yes, love, of course." The prince added, "Yes, love…whatever that is." And so the wedding was held.

The royal subjects came from all over the land to see the beautiful Princess Diana. The prince wasn't very handsome, and he wasn't very forthcoming, but he didn't seem mean at all. The subjects had always liked the prince, but they had never been nearly so fond of him as they were of his new bride. The royal wedding was the grandest wedding that ever took place in the whole world. Everyone was happy, and the princess was more radiant than ever. People came from all over the world to attend the wedding.

Soon a prince was born. His name was William. Then a second son was born whom they named Harry. They were beautiful like their mother, with golden hair and lovely smiles. Like their mother, they loved to play and have fun. And like their mother, they had a wonderful, active sense of humor.

The princess took it upon herself to go out among the people. She visited the sick, fed the hungry, housed the homeless, helped raise money for the downtrodden. She was always devoting time and energy to her royal subjects. She was also always laughing, smiling, and walking into the crowds of people who came to see her. She loved to meet and speak with people. Wherever she went, throngs gathered just to glimpse her.

Soon the royal family began to get irked. The queen told her son that he must pull in the reins on his wife, or the people would think she should run the country when the time came for the prince to rule. The prince tried to correct his wife's behavior. He scolded her for not being more reserved among their subjects, for not appearing more serious. He even scolded her in public. The prince began resenting her and resenting how much the people loved her. Everywhere they went, the royal subjects crowded to see the princess but not the prince. If the prince wanted any attention in public, he had to appear by himself, and then the crowds were much smaller than when the princess was with him.

The royal couple bickered and argued and fought. It was clear, even in public, that the princess was unhappy. She was being told to "remember her station," and to "act like a princess, not an ordinary person." Soon she fell into despair. The prince began to see another woman. Finally, the prince and princess separated, and then they divorced, with much scandal.

The princess ran away, looking for happiness anywhere she could find it. The people wished her well. Even after she was no longer the princess, they still called her "Princess Diana," and they were still more interested in seeing a former princess than they were in seeing a current prince.

The princess had many affairs, none of them very gratifying. Then she met a man who came from a similar situation. He came from a family of merchants who wanted him to take over the family business and make even more money. He wasn't interested in doing that. He just wanted to live quietly and have fun and be among the people, not sitting behind a desk long hours into the night, counting money and thinking up new ways to make more money. The princess and her new friend were quite happy together. They considered each other "soul mates." They understood each other perfectly. Finally, the princess took charge of her life and was going to be happy. She would marry her new suitor. She decided to go to the castle, where her children were visiting their father, and tell them the good news.

On the way to see her children, the princess was chased by reporters and photographers who were trying to get pictures of the princess and her new suitor that they could sell for lots of money to newspapers and magazines. They chased the car the princess and her friend were riding in. They raced through the streets at lightning speed, and suddenly there was an accident and the princess and her new friend were killed.

The whole world was stunned. People wept openly in the streets. Subjects came from all over the land to stand outside the gates of the house where the princess lived. They brought so many flowers to lay at the princess' gate that no more flowers could be found for sale in the entire kingdom. People came from every country in the world to attend the princess' funeral. And the world wept for days and days, and nothing was ever the same again.

THE INNER MEANING

If we look at this modern myth in an interpretive way, we can see how Diana was, indeed, the modern handless maiden. She was chosen, as others in her family before her, to be offered up in return for wealth and status and favor. She married the future king and was virtually sold into slavery. She was told not to be who she really was but to adopt a persona that was more acceptable to the royal family. She was ordered not to mix so openly with the commoners. She was told how to act, what to think, and how to behave. In other words, she was told not to express the feelings which came to her so naturally.

When she rebelled, when she "ran away from the castle" through divorce, we loved her all the more. She was doing what we find so difficult to do for ourselves, individually or collectively. She was standing up for the feeling function not only in herself but in all of us. Only when we cast aside our practical considerations (or try to balance them by reaching into the river of our soul to retrieve the most vulnerable part of ourselves) do we restore ourselves to wholeness.

And so we wanted her to succeed. We urged her on, encouraged her to do whatever it took to find happiness. We hoped she would ignore everything the palace said, everything anyone said that would result in her not "being herself." Yet, unaware as we may have been, we were helping in chopping off her hands by buying the very publications that were paying millions of dollars for the photographs taken by the people who were making her life so miserable. We were sacrificing her; just like her family, just like the prince.

It was more important for us to live out our feeling function through her—that is, to make her pay the price for our inability to activate our own feeling function—than to simply let her be and to turn our attentions inward and try to heal our own wounded feeling function. We asked her to carry our feeling function for us. And in doing so, she died.

Just when it looked as if she might find happiness, just when it appeared she might restore herself to wholeness, at the moment when she was dipping her silver hands into the river to save that part of herself that is represented by her children—the most tender, delicate, sensitive, and vulnerable aspects of the feeling function—her life was snuffed out by people trying to make money off her. And is it not even more ironic that the driver of the automobile was himself apparently trying to dull his own feeling function with drugs and alcohol?

TRUE TRAGEDY

There is a contemporary tendency toward the loss of true meaning in much of our language, and it results in unclear understanding of who and what we are, both individually and collectively. One word in particular comes to mind, having been altered in common parlance from its true meaning. It is the word "tragic." We use the word *tragic* to describe any sad event. A baby falling down a well is tragic; the crash of an airliner or even a dog run over by a truck might be described by news media these days as tragic. The classical definition of the word, however, is quite different.

In its original sense, a tragic situation is a situation in which a noble character acting heroically is brought to a catastrophic end through his or her own virtuous action. Hamlet is a classic example of a tragic character. He doesn't want to commit the sin of murder. He is loathe to wrong his stepfather, if indeed his stepfather is innocent of the murder of which Hamlet suspects him. Hamlet procrastinates until he thinks he knows with certainty that his stepfather poisoned his real father. In acting with such virtue, however, he waits too long. His virtue results in others being dragged into the wicked king's web, and many people, including Hamlet, die as a result. Hamlet's end is "tragic": His goodness brought about his downfall.

Diana likewise brought about her own downfall. In trying to be true to herself by following her soul, she inadvertently contributed to her own demise. By reaching out and being among her people, she was undone by the monarchy. The irony here may be that the people's very need for a monarchy was part of her undoing. The masses need a leader, but often the leader must be served up in some sacrificial manner before the needs of the people are met; that is, before any true understanding of the inner world can be achieved.

Our word "tragedy" comes from the Greek. It is literally translated as "goat song": *Tragos*, goat, plus *oide*, ode or song. It is often hypothesized that the reason the word *tragedy* came about is because the early Greek actors and singers often wore goatskins to represent satyrs. I would hypothesize a different reason. I believe the Greeks understood that any leader must, like the finest goat, be sacrificed in order for the people to survive. The leader must, like a scapegoat, take on the sins of his people, must carry their darkness into light for them, if they are to learn how to care for themselves.

Thus, every leader of true heroic stature comes to a tragic end, if not by losing her or his life literally the way Hamlet and Diana did, then by losing her or his life in some inner way, as Diana refused to do. Every monarch relinquishes a normal personal or private life in order to serve his or her subjects. But no human can live forever on the archetypal level. Diana, unlike most monarchs, sacrificed her outer world in order to remain true to the inner world, which she understood was the more important. It was the lesson she taught her people, and it exacted the ultimate price: her physical life. Which brings us to another sad element in this modern myth, this modern day tragedy: the loss of aristocracy.

Aristocracy also comes from the Greek: *aristos*, meaning "best," is joined with *kratos*, which means "rule, power, or strength." Thus, in forming an aristocracy we seek to be ruled by the best people in our midst. The good king is an archetype of the "best" among us. In the case of the inner world, the good king is the best "within" us—our enlightened ego, in the best scenario.

Collectively, we have lost our aristocrats. We look for them everywhere, project them onto the strangest people, such as movie stars, musicians, even politicians. But the truth is that true aristocrats are made from the inside out, not the other way around. Our "best leaders" are those who rise among us through their own goodness, not because we project goodness onto them. Diana was a true aristocrat.

Princess Diana led us to find within ourselves the compassionate, the beautiful, the kind, and the giving. She taught us by example to be true to our inner selves and to suffer whatever pain might be necessary in order to live with virtue. She taught us, also by example, to stand up to an evil or corrupt monarchy that insists on not doing the inner work but on being whatever it is that the outer world seems to demand, rather than being what the people truly need. Being popular is not true leadership.

True leadership divines the need of the people (which, of course, is never very different from the inner need of the leader), and then provides the model for its subjects to emulate. A true leader, a true aristocrat, is distinct from the people, of course. How else can one lead if one is not somehow recognized as different? But a true leader is never separate from his people.

Unfortunately, sometimes, as was the case with Hamlet and Princess Diana, the leader must be sacrificed in order for the people to learn how to take care of themselves. Sometimes aristocracy is truly tragic. But if we learn only the outer lessons, then we fail our leader by not paying attention to the real meaning of her life and doing our own inner work as a result. If, after watching the Princess of Wales be sacrificed for following her true nature, her true nobility, we do not learn how to pay attention to our own inner worlds and follow our own true natures, then she has not failed us, but we have failed ourselves.

The same week that Princess Diana died, Mother Teresa, a living saint, also died. She had spent her entire life selflessly serving the poor and the dying in the streets of Calcutta. There was outrage on the part of many that her death was not handled with the same intensity as that of Princess Diana. But how could it be? Why should it be? In Mother Teresa we found the "Good Mother," going about the work she loved, doing what she wanted to be doing. This woman, although she had nothing of material worth, was happy in her life. She had already found herself by looking into the inner world, where things hold together, rather than the outer world, where things fall apart or are destroyed by others. Mother Teresa's feeling function was always intact. So what was there for the world to feel bad about? We could feel sadness about her death, but devastation at the death of a saint who was living the life she wanted to live? That has no reason about it.

We were devastated by Princess Diana's death because she was us. She was the embodiment of the feeling function within each of us individually and all of us collectively. She was the vehicle by which we could relate to our feeling function. We wanted her to succeed. We wanted her to be happy. We thought that if she could be happy, we would be happy. If she could heal herself, we could be healed. But that is because we tend to make the same mistake over and over, both as individuals and as a species. We tend to confuse the outer world with the inner world.

As we have stronger and stronger reactions to people, places, things, and events in the world around us, we lose our ability to relate to ourselves; to remember that the outer world is only a mirror, reflecting what goes on in the inner world inside us. We forget that *it's never about what it's about*.

CHAPTER SEVEN

PLEASURE, HAPPINESS, AND JOY

The oddest and (at first) most disorienting thing happens to you when you know you are going to die soon, if you begin to do the work of looking inside yourself: After a while, you begin to notice that you are happy; perhaps happier than you have ever been in your life.

This experience usually comes shortly after you quit work. Leaving the workplace and structuring your days the way you want them structured, instead of the way the organization or your boss structures them for you, is an amazingly liberating experience. Don't get me wrong; it isn't easy. It takes a lot of struggling to come to the point where you can accept that you are on your own. At first, you feel guilty for not being at work. After all, aren't we all raised to be productive citizens? And when you are home every day, you aren't productive in the eyes of society. You aren't contributing to the Gross Domestic Product.

In this situation it's quite difficult, but extremely important, to understand a major point as soon as possible: There's a very good reason for not working. You're ill; that's why you're not back at the factory attaching bumpers to Mercury Montegos. There is no shame in not working when you are unable to work, and once this is comprehended, you begin to do the things you want to do. You walk the dog on the beach, go to bargain matinees, take naps. Eventually, you wake up one morning, whistle as you put on the coffee, stand on the back porch looking at the trees, or lean out your front window watching the morning traffic below, and you realize something: You're happy.

You enjoy your life. You enjoy having the day to yourself, being able to do what you want when you want—or to do nothing at all. Maybe some days you wake up tired or not feeling well. So you spend the day inside. You stay in bed or curl up on the sofa and watch old movies. You brew yourself a pot of tea. You pamper yourself. You are the only person who decides how you spend your day, and that in itself makes you happy.

After a time, you probably join a support group or seek individual therapy. There you begin to encounter all the feelings inside you. You admit you're afraid, you don't want to die, and perhaps most importantly, you don't know what to say to others about your own terminal illness. (That could be a book in itself.) But eventually you begin coming to terms with all these things. In the meantime, people are dropping all around you.

Your friends are dying. Acquaintances are dying. The daily newspaper is filled with obituaries of people who have died in this age of AIDS, half of them in their 20s and early 30s. Death is everywhere. You feel as if you're living in a concentration camp. Then one of your close friends gets seriously ill. She has no one to help, so you go to her. Before you know it, you're taking her to doctor appointments, doing the shopping, walking the dog, cleaning the house, and holding her head three times a day as she vomits up the toxic medications that are supposed to make her feel better. You're not so sure you're happy anymore, but now you rarely have time to think about your own life.

This goes on for weeks, months even. She grows worse, enters the hospital, is treated, gets better, goes home. Now she's taking care of herself. A miracle! She's going to Hawaii. Never felt better. Modern medicine, what can you say?

Three months later, she's confined to bed, weighs 90 pounds, and has more tubes and wires running through her than your home entertainment center. You care for her again, this time around the clock. Six weeks later, she dies. Bingo! In one second it's over, and your life suddenly changes again. Now you can go home, put yourself back together. You clean your own house (which hasn't been swept in seven weeks), call your friends, who haven't heard from you in several days, and cry for hours at a time.

A couple of days later, you're sitting in the kitchen having your morning coffee and taking the 23 pills you have to swallow before you start your day, and you notice something unusual. Something perplexing. Something bizarre. In the middle of this nightmare, in the middle of grieving the death of your friend and your own debilitating illness, you feel deeply satisfied and empowered. You feel strong. You are wracked with grief, as well as physical and emotional exhaustion; yet your entire being is filled with a deep and almost overwhelming sense of joy. How is this possible?

I believe this happens because it is in these times of crisis when we come fully alive. Our entire being, all our resources—physical, emotional, spiritual—are called upon to fully participate in the human experience. And in so doing we bring the wholeness and the richness of all of life to full consciousness. I believe that consciousness is joy.

BLISS

There is a basic misunderstanding in the West about the Eastern concept of bliss or nirvana. It is best exemplified in meditation classes that are found throughout Europe and the United States these days. Most often you will hear that "meditation is good for you." "Meditation will reduce stress." "Meditation lowers your blood pressure." I even saw a flyer once that read, "Learn how to make money through meditation!"

Well, all those things may be true. In fact, I see them happen all the time to people who meditate regularly. But those are hardly the reasons one should meditate, and I'm not so sure those are the best things to be thinking while a person is meditating, at least not in a truly yogic practice of meditation and without the true understanding of what those things mean on a spiritual level.

The majority of people in India or China, for example, meditate in order to transcend the world. One meditates in order to experience nothingness, not to get a new Oldsmobile. Low blood pressure and an easing of stress surely come to the person who tries to sit quietly and think of nothing, but it is not considered the end of meditation; it is not why one sits. If it is, then that is probably all one thinks about during meditation. "Is my stress level falling? Does my blood pressure feel like it's going down? Is this working?"

Likewise, bliss is not a feeling. It is not an overwhelming sense of love, a desire to run through the streets kissing everyone you meet. If that is all that happens as a result of meditation, then you also need a good therapist. Sitting is experiencing nothing. That's right: nothing—the nothing that is "ego-less." You go somewhere outside yourself, outside and beyond your ego identification, and when that happens you experience "nothingness." Sometimes it results in what is called an "out-of-body experience." I have had only one out-of-body experience, and the very instant I realized I was having it (that is, the very instant I used the word "I," as in "Oh, wow, I'm having an out-of-body experience"), it disappeared. It vanished because I had come back into myself and thought of myself as me, apart from the universe at large.

If you sit quietly and think of nothing often enough, the world begins to look quite different to you when you're through sitting and step outside. Sometimes you don't realize it until long after you sit. You simply feel different. You're calmer; things don't get on your nerves quite so easily; the noise of the street seems louder and more jarring; people seem to be saying things that don't seem very important, and they argue over the most trivial differences.

This is similar to what happens to you when you're told you are going to die and you begin to look at your inner selves and see who you really are and what you consider to be important. You look at the beautiful and the ugly; the nice and the nasty; both love and hate. And there it all is, right inside you and all around you. The world is filled with those things. You don't try to get rid of any of it; you simply take it all in and become aware of it. And as you become aware of all that exists—holiness and horror, child-birth and murder, terror and tranquility—you find you are filled with this same sensation, this same experience: joy.

It isn't a feeling; it isn't just a knowledge or an awareness. It is all these things brought together into one. It is full consciousness of what it means to be. The overwhelming richness and depth of that experience is what is often referred to as bliss. It doesn't feel good. It doesn't feel bad. It has little or nothing to do with feeling at all. It is consciousness, being fully conscious of life, all of life. That, I believe, is bliss. That is joy. It comes when we fully participate in the human experience—body, mind, heart and soul. Sometimes that means wiping the shit from incontinent friends (or strangers, for that matter) on their deathbeds. Sometimes it means holding a person's hand as she breathes her last, labored, excruciatingly painful breath. More accurately, it means taking care of her day in and day out until she takes her last breath. Take it from one who knows; there is nothing that will more surely bring you right into the center of life's true meaning than tending the dying. That honor, that holiness and horror, that deepest, most meaningful experience cannot be conveyed in words here or anywhere else. But that is bliss. That is full consciousness. That is truly living.

PLEASURE

Pleasure involves indulging the senses: touch, sight, smell, sound, taste. Your lips on your lover's lips. Seeing Renoir's *Luncheon of the Boating Party*. The aroma of freshly baked bread. Listening to a Bach cantata in a room with perfect acoustics. The richest pastry on your tongue. That is pure pleasure. It is physical, exhilarating, and ephemeral.

HAPPINESS

Happiness is a feeling of lightness or contentedness. It has to do with emotions. You meet a good friend you haven't seen for years. You love your job and go to it every day looking forward to its challenges. You win the lottery and feel secure in the knowledge that you will never be poor again. Happiness means you are content, you feel good. It, too, is ephemeral.

JOY

Joy is something else. Joy brings together all the experiences of living as a human being on the material plane so that you know with utter certainty how truly wonderful and how truly horrible life can be. You experience it totally in a split second, sometimes longer if you've been following a spiritual practice that allows you to let go of your ego when it is appropriate. This experience transcends feeling, but it involves feeling. The closest I can come to it in an analogy is this: Remember when you were a student and you struggled over a mathematics problem or a philosophical concept, but you just couldn't get the answer? It drove you insane. You walked around for days thinking of nothing but the problem in all its aspects. You stayed awake nights trying to figure it out. Then one morning as you were washing your face at the sink, it dawned on you. The answer came to you as if you were suddenly remembering a dream you had the night before. You were exhilarated, happier than you could remember being in a long time. Even your body shuddered slightly with a rush of excitement. You finally had it. All of a sudden, you knew the answer. And then the moment was gone.

After the moment passed you still knew the answer, but the moment of recognition, that split second of sheer bliss, faded. Gone is the split second when all your feelings, all your knowledge, all your days and nights of struggle and anguish came together and you clearly saw the answer. You now know the answer, and you also realize that without the struggle and mental anguish you went through in trying to figure out the answer, you would never have arrived at this moment, but the experience is no longer with you. You are left with only a memory of what it was like. (I've heard that this is similar to what happens to people who have near-death experiences. They experience what is on the other side of life, and then they are brought back and spend the rest of their lives longing for that experience of bliss.)

You never forget that moment. You're not sure you would want to go through the struggle of trying to solve the problem again, but you sure would like to relive that moment of bliss. But you can't feel that moment of bliss again unless you go through the difficult process. That is no more possible than it is to get from San Francisco to Los Angeles without traveling the three hundred miles in between. Because without making the journey from the ordinary place where we are to the extraordinary place we are striving to be, we simply can't arrive at that wonderful moment of bliss.

So when life is difficult and we feel like nothing is going right or we are so unhappy we feel as if we want to die, it might help to remember that these feelings are part of living a human existence. They come to everyone on earth. And while we may not be getting pleasure at the moment and we may not feel happy about our situation, if we can see it as part of the journey of getting from the ordinary state of mind we are normally in to the extraordinary state of mind we want to be in, then our experience will eventually be transformed into one of joy. We will experience our life as full and meaningful, even when it hurts.

CHAPTER EIGHT

THE PROCESS IS THE PRODUCT

What are you thinking right at this very moment? Ideally, you are thinking about what you are reading as you read it. However, you may very well be thinking about something else, such as the fight you had with your partner this morning. You could easily be thinking about what you're going to fix for dinner this evening. Or your mind may simply be wandering here and there, not interested by what you are reading. How many times have you caught yourself reading something and realized that you had no idea what was said in the paragraph you just read? We've all done that at one time or another.

But how many times have you actually spent an hour that way, or a full day? How many of us are spending most of our lives thinking about the past, worrying about the future, and missing what is going on in the present? There are times when I am driving down a long stretch of highway and suddenly realize I haven't been paying attention to the road ahead of me or the traffic around me. It's frightening.

So how about life in general? How many of us work at jobs we don't like in order to earn the money to pay rent and support our families? Probably most of us. It is a virtuous thing to sacrifice one's self for those we love. Yet how often do we tell ourselves we're just going to work until the car is paid off and then we're going to look for a new job? Surely we've all said to ourselves, "I'm counting the days until I go on vacation." But what about all the time, all the energy, all the activity that goes on between now and then? Buddhists have a very wise saying: Do not sacrifice the present for the future.

How many of us spend our entire lives missing out on the process of living because we're busy thinking about the product we want at the end of it? To have money, to have children, to possess notoriety and fame are all intriguing goals for one to set. But the fifty, sixty, or seventy years in between setting our goals and attaining them are easily lost by thinking only of where we are going rather than where we are at the moment. What happens to all the moments in between?

When I was younger I used to submit my poems and stories to magazines, and when I got a rejection slip back in the mail, I would tack it up on my wall. I had dozens of them. One day, a friend of mine who is also a writer saw them and asked me why I was saving them. I told him I wanted to see how many I got before I received my first acceptance letter.

"And then what?" he asked.

"Then I'll really be a writer, and I can take all these and burn them," I answered smugly. (It wasn't until years later that I realized that had been my Bad Father speaking.)

My friend laughed and shook his head. "A writer is someone who writes, my friend, not someone who publishes."

It was one of the wisest things anyone ever said to me. For years after that, I had a sign above my desk that read in big bold letters A WRITER IS SOMEONE WHO WRITES. Knowing and believing that changed everything about writing for me. I stopped writing for imaginary readers. I stopped wondering if it would please this or that editor. Realizing that I was a writer no matter what happened to the material after I wrote it freed me to listen to my heart and to write whatever I wanted, however I wanted to write it. Not surprisingly, it was only a few months after my friend's advice that I published my first poem.

THE PRICE OF THE PRODUCT

If I write to "produce a book," I am always looking to the end of my process, always directing part of my attention to some time in the future. If I write simply because I love to write, then I am completely in the moment. There's a big difference.

Focusing on the product is something we do all the time. There is a huge price to pay for that way of living. How many people get married so they can "be married," not "single" and "alone," and then realize they aren't happy living their daily lives with the person they married?

We all know someone who has left a job she loved in order to take another job because it paid more or it had a title with more prestige or because it was in a city where she always dreamed of living. Most likely, she eventually found she didn't like her new job at all. In other words, in spite of her title, her money, and her location, she didn't enjoy each minute of her day working for her new employer. So in order to achieve something (title, money, dream address), this person gave up her moment-by-moment existence. She was looking forward to the change, but she wasn't paying attention to the here and now, where she was actually quite content.

I have so many friends who go to the gym and work and work and work to make their bodies beautiful. They starve themselves, forego "fun" food, run five miles a day (even in the rain), spend hours fretting in front of the mirror. When they finally achieve the body they want they invariably come to me and ask why they aren't happy. I always say, "But I thought you loved exercising." Of course, it turns out they don't love exercising at all, but they want the results of exercising so they can feel good about themselves. But when they achieve their product—those bulging biceps, titillating triceps, and popular pectorals—they find they don't feel good about themselves anyway.

I point out to these friends that they got exactly the product they were trying to produce. If they didn't enjoy the process of producing it, then all those hours, days, weeks, months, years of lifting weights and doing sit-ups are now lost forever. Why? Because during their exercise routine, they were miserable completing 200 sit-ups. They weren't thinking about loving the sit-ups they were engaged in; they were thinking of what they would look like someday in the future in order to rationalize being miserable in the present moment.

I think exercise is essential for everyone, but I also believe we should find a form of exercise that we enjoy doing. If you enjoy being uncomfortable and find meaning and fulfillment in it, then by all means, engage in it. Otherwise, find some way to spend your time and energy that is meaningful to you. If you have a cerebral hemorrhage in the middle of your sit-ups, will your last thought be, "I'm so happy I'm dying doing sit-ups?"

If we don't like what we're doing, we usually aren't going to like what it gets us. Here again, it's never about what it's about. Look at these situations and see if any of them are familiar.

- The woman who spends night after night at the singles bar and still can't find the right partner.

- The young man who studies law for six years because he wants to have a fabulous house, a red Porsche, and date beautiful people, but who is depressed for the six years it takes to get through school.

- The painter who rushes to finish the paintings he needs in order to have enough work to enter an exhibit, and who is nervous and can't sleep for weeks.

- The parent who spends half a lifetime manipulating her children into becoming doctors or actors or attorneys only to watch them move across the country after they graduate and proceed to have a life that doesn't include her.

Many people will read this and think that it's worth it. They will say, "So what if you have to give up six years of your life to become a lawyer? Look at what you get after that." It might be more accurate to say, "Look at what you hope you'll get after that." Perhaps the question we might ask is, "What will you become as a result of what you do?"

In almost every instance you can cite, if you look beyond what is going on at surface level, you will find that it's never about what it's about. My old friend Connie, an aspiring opera singer, used to say, "If you want to get at the truth of a person's character, just turn down the volume and watch the picture for a while." Like Aristotle, she believed that you know a thing by what it does. You know a person by what she does, as well. So what might really be going on with the people in the situations listed above?

The woman at the singles bar is looking for the right person. She just hasn't been able to find the one who will make her feel special. All she wants is love and respect, fidelity and devotion. She wants to feel good about her life. And don't we all? It isn't really a person she's looking for; it's a feeling, a state of mind, a tranquillity of spirit. She wants to love herself, respect herself. If she could attain that, she would realize she doesn't need anyone else. She may want a girlfriend or a boyfriend or a lover, but she doesn't need one to be happy. What she needs is to do some inner work. She would be better off spending her evenings doing some deep introspection rather than looking for her dream lover. Self esteem isn't something that comes from the outside. It can come only from within. If one doesn't possess it, no one else can give it to you.

Our young law student doesn't want to be a lawyer; he wants to have all the prestige and status that he sees lawyers granted in our society. He doesn't want to practice law; he wants to drive a snazzy sports car and have beautiful people all around him. These are the "products" he can attain after his six-year process of law school. Why doesn't it occur to him that those six years are also important? Why is it that so much valuable time in his life is expendable? Does it never occur to him that he might be able to have some of the products he hungers for by spending those six years becoming expert at something he loves doing rather than something that holds no deep meaning for him? Wouldn't he be better off throwing his heart and soul into something he can feel passionate about?

Our painter has probably been working in his studio for years. A chance comes to be part of an exhibit or to have a one-person show, but the gallery owner wants ten pieces just like the ones he has painted in the past six months. He only has four. So he works night and day to finish another six within the next six months. Those six months are a living hell for him and everyone around him. He is exhausted, run-down, irritable. He fights with his partner almost every night after working from dawn till dusk. When it's over, he has six more paintings that he feels somewhat ambivalent about; six paintings that contain and exude the frustration, anger, and desperation he felt while painting them. He hates looking at them, even though they are considered good by others. What if he had dropped dead in the middle of those six months? Would he have died doing what he loved doing? Would he have thought the process was worth the product?

What about the last person on our list? You don't have to be a parent to relate to this one: manipulating people to do something you want them to do. In the case of parents, it's usually something they always longed to do but never had the opportunity to do. The young law student we discussed previously might very well have been doing what he was taught he should do. His parents may have sacrificed everything to put their son through law school. There are no guarantees that when he finishes he will want anything to do with his parents. In the meantime, what is going on in the process? How many arguments, how many tearful nights? How many days of worrying and fretting?

DON'T DRINK THE WATER

Why don't we think our moment-by-moment lives are valuable? Why aren't they precious to us? It's such a mystery. Is it because we all think we are never going to die? That we will live forever? There is a wonderful story in the *Mahabharata* of India. After a fierce battle between two warring families, twelve princely warriors in exile in the forest come, one by one, upon a river. Each is fatigued and thirsty after fighting for many days and nights. As each one arrives he kneels down to drink, and as he does he hears a voice say, "Don't drink the water." Each man, in turn, looks around, sees no one, and begins to drink again. Again he hears the voice. "Don't drink the water."

But each man ignores the voice and drinks. And each man dies. Finally, the leader of the family, named Yudisthira, comes to the river bank. There, spread out along the shore are a dozen of his beloved brothers, uncles, and cousins, all dead. He begins to wail and to implore God. The voice resounds again, but this time it says,"Yudisthira, answer me this question and I will restore life to these men."

"Yes, yes, anything, Lord. Ask me."

"Yudisthira, what is the most amazing and perplexing phenomenon in the universe?"

"That is easy, Lord," Yudisthira answers humbly. "The most amazing and perplexing phenomenon in the universe is that although we see our grandparents and parents die of old age, sisters and wives die during childbirth or of some mysterious illness, our brothers, cousins, and friends die in battle all around us, each one of us believes in his heart that he will never die. Each human being secretly believes he will live forever."

And with that correct answer, God restores the lives of the men of Yudisthira's family, who were too proud to listen to a voice they couldn't see and who believed they would live forever.

YOU ONLY HAVE WHAT'S INSIDE YOU

There's a surefire question to ask if you want to know if your life is meaningful to you. Ask yourself this:

If I knew I was going to die this evening, would I spend the day doing what I'm doing?

If the answer is "yes," then you are probably living a conscious and joyful life, whether you are a senator or a seamstress. If the answer is "no," then the next step is to ask yourself what you would be doing if you knew this was the last day of your life—and then find a way to spend the rest of your life doing it.

What we get at the end of the day may be materially attractive. It may make all our friends and acquaintances envious. It may even be exactly what we have always dreamed we wanted to achieve. But if we don't have meaning throughout the day, if we aren't engaged in activity that fulfills us and gives us joy, aren't those hours lost? What if you had died at 1:15 this afternoon? Would your last words have been, "I'm so happy, so fulfilled. I always hoped I'd die like this?"

When a person believes she's going to die within a given amount of time, the present becomes all she has. When a man is told his heart is very weak and he could keel over dead at any moment, he starts choosing very carefully how he spends his time. My friend Pete is the perfect example of someone who learned this and taught it to me. I have never forgotten it.

About four months before Pete became bedridden with AIDS, he did something he had always wanted to do but had never been able to afford. He bought himself a brand-new car. It was big, beautiful, and burgundy. Pete loved that car so much it was almost embarrassing. He drove it everywhere, even to the corner store. He would stand at the window of his living room looking out at it. He polished that car so much he had carpal tunnel syndrome.

When Pete was too weak to walk unassisted, he would ask me to help him to the front of the house, where he would sit for a while and look at his car. When he was unable to get up even with assistance, he asked me to take several photos of the car, which he kept near his bed. About a month before he died, Pete looked at me one evening as I was sitting with him and said, "There's something you must remember after I'm gone."

I was instantly curious as to what he would say. I thought perhaps he was going to tell me where he had hidden some money or that I was to deliver a message to someone. I assured him I would remember and took his hand. "What is it?" I asked.

"At the very end of your life, all you have is what you think and how you feel. It doesn't matter if you live in a mansion or in a cardboard box under a bridge. At the very end, you have nothing except what's inside you."

Pete learned not to confuse the product with the process and spent the end of his life trying to smooth out rough relationships, getting to the bottom of some of his emotional problems, and reading thought-provoking books. When Pete died that December, he died a fairly happy man. He was 36.

I learned three things from Pete and from others in my life who have died slow, thoughtful deaths:

1) We are alive to live.
2) The process of living is the product of living.
3) There is nothing we are here to make, to become, or to achieve.

The secret of life is to live it consciously, paying attention to each and every moment. Life takes its meaning from the concerted effort of body, heart, mind, and soul. Those wise, ancient Hindus knew the secret. The secret to attaining bliss is to think always of God and remember your own death.

I wonder if that was their way of saying that in life, the process is the product?

CHAPTER NINE

THE "G" WORD

Even though it is currently politically incorrect in sophisticated circles to use the "G" word, you have no doubt noticed that Paul and I use it throughout this book. Sometimes we use other words in its place, but there should be no doubt when you see these words that we are speaking of what humankind most commonly refers to as "God."

Before you break into a cold sweat, hear me out. This doesn't require that you use the word, but I want you to know what is meant by it. Most of what I believe about God can be summed up in two quotations from two ancient texts. Once again, they come from the Hindu tradition.

In the first excerpt God has disguised himself as a chariot driver. He is a servant to a young prince named Arjuna. At a crucial point in Arjuna's young life, God—known in this text as Krishna—reveals himself in all his glory to Arjuna. Arjuna, understandably, is shocked and terrified. The following is some of what Krishna says to the young prince, who is crouching inside the chariot in absolute astonishment.

Gita, Book IX, 13-34 and X, 20

"Those who realize true wisdom,
rapt within this clear awareness,
see me as the universe's
origin, imperishable.

All their words and actions
issue from the depths of worship;
held in my embrace, they know me
as a woman knows her lover.

Creatures rise, creatures vanish;
I alone am real, Arjuna,
looking out, amused, from deep
within the eyes of every creature.

I am the object of all knowledge,
Both father of the world, its mother,
source of all things, of impure and
pure, of holiness and horror.

I am the goal, the root, the witness,
home and refuge, dearest friend,
creation and annihilation,
everlasting seed and treasure.

I am the radiance of the sun, I
open or withhold the raincloud,
I am immortality and
death, am being and non-being.

I am the Self, Arjuna, seated
in the heart of every creature.
I am the origin, the middle,
and the end that all must come to.

Those who worship me sincerely
with their minds and bodies, giving
up their whole lives in devotion,
find in me their heart's fulfillment.

Even those who do not know me,
if their actions are straightforward,
just, and loving, venerate me
with the truest kind of worship.

All your thoughts, all your actions,
all your fears and disappointments,
offer them up to me, clear-hearted;
know them all as passing visions.

Thus you free yourself from bondage,
from both good and evil karma;
through this path of non-attachment, you
embody me, in utter freedom.

I am justice: clear, impartial,
favoring no one, hating no one.
But in those who have cured
themselves of
selfishness, I shine with brilliance.

Even murderers and rapists,
tyrants, the most cruel fanatics,
ultimately know redemption
through my love, if they surrender

to my harsh but healing graces.
Passing through excruciating
transformations, they find freedom
and their hearts find peace within them.

I am always with all beings;
I abandon no one. And
however great your inner darkness,
you are never separate from me.

Let your thoughts flow past you, calmly;
keep me near, at every moment;
trust me with your life, because I
am you, more than you yourself are."

In India, among Hindus, God is referred to as the Self, with a capital "S," as opposed to the word self with a small "s," which refers to an individual.

From the *Kena Upanishad*:

The Self is the ear of the ear, the eye of the eye. It is the mind of the mind, the speech of speech, and the life of life. Not clinging to any of the senses, not attached to any thought in the mind, the wise become one with the deathless Self.

Eye cannot see It, tongue cannot utter It, mind cannot grasp It. There is no way to learn or to teach It. It is different from the known, beyond the unknown. In this all the ancient Masters agree.

That which makes the tongue speak but which cannot be spoken by the tongue—that alone is God, not what people worship.

That which makes the mind think but which cannot be thought by the mind—that alone is God, not what people worship.

That which makes the eye see but which cannot be seen by the eye—that alone is God, not what people worship.

That which makes the ear hear but which cannot be heard by the ear—that alone is God, not what people worship.

If you think that you know God, you know very little; all that you can know are ideas and images of God.

I do not know God, nor can I say that I don't know It. If you understand the meaning of "I neither know nor don't know," you understand God.

Those who realize that God cannot be known, truly know; those who claim that they know, know nothing.

The ignorant think that God can be grasped by the mind; the wise know It is beyond knowledge.

When you see that God acts through you at every moment in every movement of mind or body, you attain true freedom. When you realize the truth, and cling to nothing in the world, you enter eternal life.

I was raised as a Catholic. When I reached the age of 18 and went off to college, I gradually stopped practicing the Catholic religion. I did so for one reason and one reason only: I could not accept any religion that thought it was the only path to God and which went so far as to exclude certain people on the basis of how they were born, namely, gay or lesbian.

I knew I was a moral person and strove to be virtuous in all my actions. I discovered I was gay when I was in my early teens. I did not decide to become gay the way one decides to dye his hair another color. To reject people because of what they are—what God made them—is, to my way of thinking, the height of arrogance and pride and is just plain mean.

I didn't practice any spiritual path for many years. Then I met my first partner, Andre, and he introduced me to meditation and a non-Western way of looking at the universe and all that is in it. Suddenly, everything came together. I felt that I experienced God for the first time. I didn't know God, but I "sensed" her within and around me.

There are two parts of the previous quotes which particularly appeal to me. When I read them something inside resonates strongly, as if to say "Yes, this is true." The first is from the *Bhagavad Gita* and it is this:

Creatures rise, creatures vanish;
I alone am real, Arjuna,
looking out, amused, from deep
within the eyes of every creature.

The other is related to it and clarifies it somewhat. It is from
the *Kena Upanishad*:

If you think that you know God, you know very little;
all that you can know are ideas and images of God.

All our lives we are shown pictures that portray God as an old
man with a long white beard or in some other material form. We
are constantly told:

- we must obey God's laws;

- God doesn't like us to do certain things, and when we do, it
  makes him angry;

- God hates certain people, such as homosexuals;

- when people die they go to hell, which is filled with fire, or
  heaven, which is paved with gold;

- if a person isn't baptized, he cannot enter heaven at all.

I could go on and on, but this short list will make the point.
These things never made sense to me, even as a child. What's
more, they felt wrong. I believe that faith is what takes over when

sense or reason fail. With things like those listed above, however, no faith I could muster made me believe they were accurate. My intuition, my gut feeling, as it were, convinced me that they were simply not true.

Whenever I encountered these attitudes I would have immediate reactions to each of them:

- I could never understand why God would have any laws at all. If God created everything and God makes no mistakes, why would God have to make laws to keep things right when creation was finished? If chaos or disorder exists, didn't God also create that? And if God did, mustn't it have some purpose, even if we can't figure out what that purpose is? Does God have to obey the laws too? Are these laws applicable everywhere in the universe?

- If God is perfection, how is it God can get angry? Only people get angry, not God. If God gets angry, does that mean God is subject to other emotions as well? Does God get jealous? Is God afraid of things? How do I know when God is in a good mood? Does God get horny too?

- Why would God hate anybody? If God brings all things into existence, why would God create something and then hate it? Does God hate white people? Does God hate people who slurp their soup? Does God hate people who worship him in ways different from the way I worship God? Or, what if I'm the one worshipping God wrongly; does that mean God hates me?

- Why would God send souls to a place with fire to punish them if souls are without substance and not subject to the same senses as the body? Why would God build mansions and pave streets with gold in a place where you won't have a body? What good are gold streets if you don't have feet with which to walk on them or eyes with which to see them?

- Does every Muslim, Hindu, Buddhist, Native American, and all the other billions of people who don't practice baptism go to hell automatically? Isn't there even one person among them who deserves to go to heaven? If not, why is God so unfair? And if God is unfair, then is God a mean, nasty, vengeful God? And if God is dishonest, why should I try to be good?

THOSE WHO THINK THEY KNOW, KNOW VERY LITTLE

The question I ultimately found myself asking was, "Why does all this sound like a human being made it up?" It was apparent that man was creating God in his own image, not the other way around.

So when I read "If you think that you know God, you know very little; all that you can know are ideas and images of God," something inside whispers "Yes!" That not only makes sense; it resonates deep within me as being true. Why would the ultimate source be anything like us? If God created space and time, doesn't God exist outside of space and time? And if God does, then why would one ever imagine that God's essence exists only within space and time? It makes no sense whatsoever.

Not only that, but one thing perplexes me even now: Why do

human beings think they can know everything? Why aren't there some things—like God—that we can admit are just too mysterious for us to grasp? Where did we get all this hubris, all this excessive pride? When I came across the concept that we can only know "ideas and images of God" in the Upanishads I found something that resonated as true.

So I'm left thinking that perhaps God isn't a person or anything even remotely like a person. Perhaps God isn't even a thing. Perhaps God is something else, something I can't even imagine. What does it matter? You either believe or you don't believe.

Maybe it doesn't even matter if I believe. Consider this passage from the Gita:

> Even those who do not know me,
> if their actions are straightforward,
> just, and loving, venerate me
> with the truest kind of worship.

There are so many things in life we don't understand, especially in the moment. Being in the thick of an emotionally charged situation, for example, is the wrong time to try to understand it. Later, however, with time and emotional distance from it, things might look different, might make some sort of sense. It's like standing with your nose right up against a painting and trying to see what the whole painting is. That's not possible. But if you slowly begin to back away (gaining time and distance from the painting), you will begin to see the whole picture. Just like life. Why can't God be like that?

I can have an idea of God; a concept that will help me to think about God. I can create an image of God so long as I remember that the image is just a representation. God not only doesn't look like the image, but doesn't even exist on the same level as the material world. This works. This places God on a level that is so transcendent, so mysterious, it makes sense that only God would exist there. And only God is smart enough to comprehend God.

WHAT IF EVERYTHING IS GOD?

Then I happened across another discussion of God in Fritjof Capra's book *The Tao of Physics*, which really got me thinking. The discussion went something like this: The universe consists mostly of space. The earth and its atmosphere is made up mostly of space. Now that we have atomic and subatomic microscopes, scientists have discovered that atoms and subatomic particles consist mostly of space. Yes, there are particles of solid matter, but they whirl around in a relatively huge space. The space between the solid matter is filled with a kind of energy. That energy is what holds everything together. It holds the atom together, which holds the object together, and so on and so on. That energy is what we refer to as God.

Once again, the inner resonance was like a voice whispering "Yes." This would mean God is in everything and everyone. When Christ said, "The kingdom of God is within," he wasn't speaking metaphorically. God is in everything. In fact, God *is* everything.

The Jewish tradition has a saying, which I will paraphrase: "Treat every traveler you meet on the road as if he were God. He just might be."

In the New Testament, Christ is quoted as saying to his followers, "Whatever you do to these, the least of thy brethren, you do unto me."

Those both sound a lot like, "Only I am real, Arjuna, looking out, amused, from deep within the eyes of every creature."

IT'S OKAY NOT TO KNOW

The point of all this is to say that when you start to delve into yourself you will find many mysteries, countless unanswerable questions. Most of them point you toward something other. When that happens, if you don't know what the "other" is, don't fret over it. It is a mystery that we cannot fully comprehend. We have ideas of It, even images of It, but we do not know It. And in knowing we don't know It, somehow we come closer to It. In being so filled with pride that we think we can know everything or in pretending to comprehend It, we just make fools of ourselves.

Why it has become fashionable to avoid God is not difficult to understand. There are two salient reasons I can think of immediately. First, those of us who were educated through college became a bit cynical. We were taught to believe nothing unless it could be proven *a posteriori*—that is, with lots of evidence to back it up. Our society worships everything that relates to the material: flesh, money, power. We want only what is perceptible by our senses. This is what we've been taught, and we have been raised in a culture that reinforces it at every turn.

Second, we have seen more violence enacted through religious fanaticism than under any other banner: Hindus killing Muslims, Muslims killing Jews, Christians killing one another because of the different ways in which they interpret the same scriptures. Then there are certain "Christians" hating and advocating the murder of homosexuals and those who believe in a woman's right to have jurisdiction over her own body. All this is done in the name of God. Is it any wonder that thoughtful, conscientious people don't want to be associated with God? Saying you believe in God is beginning to be more and more like saying you were a close friend of Adolf Hitler or that you're Saddam Hussein's bridge partner.

One of the interesting aspects of this phenomenon is that for some reason it's okay to refer to the Universe with a capital "U," invoke the name of "the Goddess," or to use some other appellation when we mean God—so long as it isn't the word "God." In times of crisis, however, I notice that 99 percent of all people—including those who eschew talking about God—begin to pray. I wonder if these people expect to be heard, and if so, by whom or what?

In critical moments the ego seems willing to give up a little room, to make room for something other than itself. I suppose that's because in times of real crisis the ego gets the message that it is not in control of everything after all. That it takes a major trauma like death, divorce, or terminal illness to convince the ego that it isn't the be-all and end-all of existence tells us a lot about human nature.

We have correct "hunches" about things all the time. We boast at being able to "know" someone after just five minutes of talking with him. We call ourselves good judges of people's character on a first encounter. Yet we're uncomfortable when we have these inexplicable feelings that there just might be more out there than we can prove. With hunches and snap judgments of character, the ego is inflated and feels smart about its knowledge of the world. But when we intuit the presence of something transcendent and beyond our capacity to comprehend, the ego is threatened. We are such funny creatures after all. We are such children in adults' clothing.

Regardless of your faith or lack of faith in a god, the observations about human life in this book can still be considered valid, still fairly universal, at least in our Western culture. That "other power" that gets talked about can even be interpreted as the human unconscious or the deepest part of the psyche. It doesn't matter what you call it; in the end we're all talking about the same thing: that unknowable mystery that once in a while we know is there. We know it *a priori*, that is, without being able to prove it. We just know. There are some things, whether the ego likes it or not, that we just know.

PRACTICE SOMETHING

My main concern for people who, like me, gave up the religious practice in which they were raised is that some form of practice be found again. It doesn't have to be part of some organized, institutionalized spiritual practice. In fact, I think most people are better off avoiding codified, politicized forms of spirituality. But we must find a way to explore spirituality and open the door to finding "God" without getting soiled by the vocabulary of religion.

Allan Watts talks about how people "feel funny" when certain words, like "God," "Jesus," or "sacrament," are used. I think he's right; I know I have strong reactions to certain Christian terminology. Jungian writer Robert A. Johnson, on the other hand, often recommends to clients that they return to the religion in which they were raised to see if there's anything there they can build upon. I have found that to be excellent advice.

I followed Johnson's suggestion at one point and went back to the Catholic church in my early forties, looking for a spiritual community within which I could worship. I found many elements of Catholicism spoke to me, and I integrated them into my own eclectic version of spiritual practice, which borrows from the Hindus, the Buddhists, and the Muslims. I find Catholic ritual very helpful indeed, especially the iconography of the saints and the Blessed Mother. Thinking of Christ as a true Boddhisattva has entirely changed my attitude toward his teachings and enabled me to hear him once again. I don't think it matters much what you try so long as you try something that will put you in touch with elements that transcend this material world.

I have truly been blessed with a few wonderful friends. For various reasons, most of them are extremely successful in their professions and have reaped remarkable financial benefits. In the past four years, every single one of them without exception—and there are seven in all—have come to me and Paul in a vale of tears, feeling their lives were falling apart in spite of all their good fortune.

Do something "other," we always tell them. Anything. Turn your focus outside yourself. Pursue a spiritual practice of some sort, even if it's worshipping your inner Self. The very ritual of devotion is such a loving act that it will open many doors for you. Whatever you choose—worship, prayer, contemplation, acts of charity, intellectual pursuits, gardening—do it with love in your heart. Do it out of respect for others and for the deepest, most mysterious part of yourself. The rest will follow, I promise.

My old teacher Muktananda used to say, "Give people the mantra. Let them say it over and over. Never mind if they don't know what it means. The mantra will do the work for them." I have actually seen that work. Just entering into a ritual with an open, well-intentioned heart will work miracles all by itself.

FAITH

Man—and although I am using the term generically, I mean it here to apply primarily to the male of the species—can't stand to think there are things in the universe that he is unable to figure out or comprehend. Since Descartes kicked God out of the center of things and placed himself and the rest of humankind in the very vortex of existence, human beings have assumed there is nothing beyond their grasp. This is, to my mind, the greatest mystery of all.

I don't believe we can know everything. I believe quite firmly that there are many things we cannot know. This is where faith comes into play. When we know something is true but we can't prove it—that is, when we know something *a priori*—this is when faith takes over. And while I cannot possibly prove that the energy between subatomic particles is God, I quite completely believe it to be true. How can that be God? Why not? Is that just my own personal metaphor for God? Why not? Does it really matter? Everyone who believes in God believes there is just one god, so no matter what we think God is, we're all worshipping the same God. Truth is in the devotee, not in the symbol being worshipped.

People argue that God is this or that. He looks like a man, a woman, a jackal. God doesn't want you to eat pig meat. God wants you to stab your son to death as an offering to prove you love him. God is invisible. God speaks only to Muslim prophets. God relays information only to old Jews on mountain tops. Sounds silly, doesn't it? Yet we kill one another over these very ideas. Why? I haven't the faintest idea.

I've never been to Mars. No one I know has ever been to Mars. Yet we all believe it is there. And each of us has a particular image in our minds when we think of Mars, its climate and its geography. I dare say that no two people carry the exact same images of Mars in their minds, yet when we say "Mars," we all know what one another means and we accept it. People don't kill one another over their different ideas or images of what Mars is or what it looks like. I say "Mars" and you say, "Oh, yeah, Mars. Right." Then I think of a red planet with a lot of dust; you think of a brown desert with little green women running around on it, and we go on with our conversation. Why can't we do that with God?

I celebrate my birthday every year for a solid week. Sometimes it goes on for two weeks. During that two-week period, I do something every day to mark my birthday. Other people celebrate their birthdays on the anniversary of the day they were born and on no other day. When I say, "My birthday is coming up," I think of a weeklong celebration. You hear the word "birthday" and think of the single day you will celebrate your birthday with a birthday cake and candles. With those images in our minds, we go on discussing birthdays. Even if I tell you how I celebrate my birthday over a long period of several days, you don't hate me for it. I don't slap you in the face when I hear you only celebrate your birthday for a single day, or perhaps not at all. Why should ideas of God be handled any differently?

If I tell you I worship God by putting on furs and feathers and burning a smudge pot in my living room on the night of the full moon, you will probably stop socializing with me. If you tell me you worship God by lighting seven candles and eating seven frogs sitting in front of a poster-sized picture of a chicken, which you believe to be an exact representation of what God looks like, I will probably not call you the next time I want company at the movies.

Why do we do this? If your chicken-god and my formless god

are just "ideas," if they are just some means for us poor mortals to get a handle on the concept of a "god," and we are practicing devotions and not hurting anyone in the process, what does it matter how we worship? Why do I feel compelled to force you to worship the same god I worship and in the same way?

The Tibetan Buddhist monk Sogyal Rinpoche said once in a lecture I heard him give that you can tell a lot about a person's spiritual beliefs by whether he has a sense of humor about them. If a person can laugh at his religion, laugh at some of the rituals or practices of his spiritual path, laugh at how silly some of his beliefs might appear on the surface, then he truly believes in his spiritual practice. If, however, a person has no sense of humor about his spiritual path, it's likely that he isn't convinced of its truthfulness himself. I think Rinpoche is on to something there.

The point of all this, I suppose, is simply to say that we all need to lighten up about a lot of things, but especially about our ideas and images of God. It's none of my concern how others worship, or even if others worship. What I do care about is that everyone is free to believe what he or she wants to believe in order to complete whatever journey he or she happens to be on in this life. I also ask the same of others. It seems so simple; yet, for some reason humans have never in their history been able to achieve it.

LIGHT A CITY OR BUILD A BOMB

"If there is a God, how can he allow so much evil and suffering in the world?" I hear this question more often than any other question about God, especially from people who say they can't believe in a God who would allow such things to exist. When these people pose the question to me, it is usually the beginning of the end of our relationship because they really don't want to hear my answer.

I always tell them, "I don't think God allows those things to happen. I believe God *is* those things happening." That usually sends them scurrying for the exit. Here's what I mean: If God is that energy I spoke of earlier and not an old man in a mansion of gold living between Pluto and Saturn who spends all day hurling some people into heaven and others into hell, then God is everything. If God is everything, then God is not only in Mother Teresa, but God is in Adolf Hitler as well. We certainly don't want to hear that. But let's think about it.

I often use the analogy of nuclear power to discuss this belief of mine that God is the energy between the subatomic particles and, therefore, God is everything. Nuclear energy can be used to build a devastating bomb that kills millions of people, or it can be used to light an entire city. How it is used is determined by the user. That energy, as directed by humans, manifests itself in numerous and different ways. Sometimes it comes out in works of mercy; other times it comes out as murder. It is the "filter" of human consciousness (or lack of consciousness) that determines how the energy manifests.

When I tripped over the dog, instead of throwing a mug, perhaps I could have done something constructive with that same energy if I had been able to stay conscious of what was happening. Not that there's anything wrong with throwing mugs—so long as you stay conscious of why you are throwing them and let all your anger out in the process. When rage is managed in that fashion, it can be appropriately directed. When we consciously and appropriately direct our anger, it is a most cathartic experience.

Humans have a tendency to judge things morally. There is a

right and a wrong, a good and an evil. But what if, outside time and space, there is no morality—no good, no evil, no right, no wrong? What if outside time and space there is only It? Energy. God. And inside Time and Space the energy exists as the energy between the subatomic particles that holds the entire universe together. Then the uses we put that energy to and the effects it has are only as good or as evil as we dictate.

You say you don't understand how that can be possible. Sometimes I'm not sure how electricity, gravity, or magnetism work, but I believe they are there. I see the effects of them all around me. What I do believe most emphatically is that there is only one God. I don't believe there is a right and a wrong way to worship that God, nor do I believe that God thinks there is. I think right and wrong are relative. What is against the law in France may not be against the law in Germany. Why? Because the people in those two countries have decided to have different criteria for determining right and wrong. People on a remote Pacific island may think that the fatter you are, the more beautiful you are. In the United States you will never see a fat person held up as an example of beauty. What one culture holds valuable and desirable another culture ridicules or condemns.

Personally, I believe God doesn't have any criteria for anything. I think God doesn't think the way humans do: right, wrong, good, bad, big, little, pretty, ugly, black, white. I think those are human concepts, like good and evil. We tend to make rules and boundaries where none exist. Have you ever flown across the United States? When you fly from California to New York, if you look out of the plane, can you see the line where Nevada ends and Utah begins? Do you see all the lines and barriers between the states? Do you see a natural line where the United States ends and Canada begins? No, of course not. The earth doesn't make those distinctions. Humans do. We impose our sense of order on the universe, and it usually ends up creating chaos where none existed before. Like my idea of God versus your idea of God. As if we didn't have more important things to worry about.

In Shivaite Hinduism, the belief is that "God lives in you as you." Not in you as some tiny cell hiding away in your heart or your liver or your brain. Not as some tiny bright light that exists in you, but is separate from you. No, God lives in you as you. That means that you are God. You just aren't aware of it. Your consciousness hasn't gotten that enlightened yet. If we are God, shouldn't we be behaving better? Shouldn't we be acting a bit more God-like?

So as you continue here and find references to God, the Universe, the Goddess, Universal Consciousness, the Ultimate Cow, the Transcendental Chicken, etc., please remember what I'm referring to. It's vague. It's elusive. It's unknowable in any empirical sense. It is bigger than all of us, smaller than any of us. I know that I don't know It; and in knowing that, I know It better than most. You probably do, too.

CHAPTER TEN

ATTACHMENT, DETACHMENT, AND NON-ATTACHMENT

I think any person who has been told she is going to die will agree that the most difficult task a person is faced with at the end of her life is "letting go." Giving up the world and its charms is nearly impossible. The human spirit struggles desperately to remain on the material plane. We call this struggle our "survival instinct," and every sentient being has an instinct to survive.

When the time comes for our lives to end, letting go of life is no longer a choice. There are so many things to let go of. Normally the first things that come to mind are one's home and possessions: our favorite painting, Aunt Cecilia's wedding ring, Dad's bomber jacket. We want to hang on to all the things in our lives that mean something to us. Think of my friend Pete and how he wanted to hang on to his new red car. It was his most prized possession. He treasured it not because it was such a wonderful thing in itself; after all, there are millions of cars out there one could own. He valued it because of the meaning he attached to it. It was a symbol of his success.

Pete had managed to escape from an abusive home at the age of 13. He was on his own for the rest of his life. Uneducated, without financial resources, he taught himself electronics and found a job at the University of California in San Francisco. He was a "tinkerer," and during his tenure at the university he invented many things. One of them was a device that helped hearing-impaired and deaf individuals to regain some, if not all, of their hearing capabilities.

Pete's car represented his triumph over adversity, his ingenuity, his individuality. The fact that he earned enough money to afford an automobile signified to him that he was truly free of any dependence on other people. The car was his reminder of that. That's why Pete loved his car so much. It's never about what it's about.

I also believe that people who are dying will tell you they have found that material things are actually the easiest to let go of. In fact, terminally ill people at some point usually begin to give things away to family and loved ones, sometimes even to strangers. There is a sense of liberation in letting go of one's possessions. It produces a feeling of having less to weigh one down, as it were, less to keep one anchored to the earth. It is like riding in a hot air balloon and throwing things overboard in order to make the balloon go higher.

The truly difficult "things" to let go of are the people we love. I have seen men and women stay alive against insurmountable odds because they did not want to leave their loved ones. I have watched friends with AIDS waste away until they were literally nothing but skin and bones, yet they would not let go of life because they did not want to leave their partners, children, or friends. It is a very painful process to watch, and, I imagine, an even more painful process to go through yourself.

What does one do to prepare for this? Ideally, we are prepared for it when the time comes because we have practiced letting go during our lifetime. But that is the ideal. I knew of only two people who lived relatively unattached to the world, and both of those individuals were attached to loved ones.

ATTACHMENT

There is no need to explain what attachment is. We are all attached to the world in many ways. We are attached to our homes, our belongings, our clothes. We would be lost without our computers and our automobiles. Think of how attached we have become to things we simply take for granted: electricity, the telephone, television. Examples of our attachment are all around us.

Under some circumstances, our attachments may diminish without our having to do anything about it. We might be confined to bed and after a while find that we stop thinking of our favorite restaurant. If we find ourselves in constant physical discomfort, before long we will give up our attachment to our weekend skiing trips or Rollerblading in the park on Sundays. Through pain and discomfort our attention becomes diverted to more immediate things. It is, perhaps, not the perfect way to abandon attachments, but it is a common and effective way nonetheless.

DETACHMENT

There are spiritual paths that teach and practice detachment. Buddhists are probably the most widely known for advocating that we give up the world and worldly things. The practice of meditation is aimed toward transcending the world, rising above the material plane. This detachment is a most severe approach to achieving an emotional and spiritual equilibrium. It strikes me as a kind of "all-or-nothing" approach to living: One is either attached to or detached from the world, with little or no room in between.

Various Christian sects and religious orders practice detachment from the world. Certain monks and nuns are cloistered away from the daily concerns of society. They have given up the ways of the world in order to pray and contemplate the mysteries of God.

The Buddha was a wealthy and powerful young prince when he left his kingdom. He abandoned all its luxuries and comforts in order to find the meaning of life. He wandered throughout the East for the rest of his life, begging for the basic necessities of his existence. He relied upon the compassion of others even for food, shelter, and clothing. Very few of us are prepared to go that far.

So now we have two options:

- attachment to the world and all it has to offer, which is usually thought of as a non-spiritual way of living;

- detachment from the world, which is usually considered the most severe form of a spiritual path.

NON-ATTACHMENT

There is a third way to live; a way which achieves equilibrium and is, to my way of thinking, a soundly balanced approach. It is, however, extremely difficult. It is practiced most often by Hindus, particularly Hindus of the Tantric tradition. The Tantric approach to life says something like this: Have everything the world has to offer and live life to the absolute fullest you possibly can, but do not become attached to any of it. This approach is called non-attachment. It does not advocate giving up everything and turning your back on the world. Quite the opposite. It encourages indulging in everything. It admonishes us, however, not to become attached to any of these pleasures but to engage in them prayerfully. Tantra makes all of life into a yoga, a prayerful practice whose end is enlightenment, or the experience of the Self.

When most Westerners visit the Hindu temples of India, they are appalled when they find countless depictions of the gods and their consorts copulating. Every temple to Shiva will have somewhere on the grounds a depiction of Shiva and Parvati in various positions of coitus. Hindus understand this act to be a most divine one. It is the union of masculine and feminine energies (as in our story of Ganesha). It is the union of two into one—the life energy at its most powerful. It is possibly the only moment outside of deep meditation when a human being loses all awareness of ego and separateness. The Hindus believe, therefore, that sex can be one of the highest forms of prayer. Can you imagine an American thinking of God while making love? Even the most uninhibited sex acts can be a prayer, if one is mindful of God during the act. In other words, everything is a prayer, if you make it so.

Spiritual masters in the Hindu and Buddhist traditions tell us that our ability to walk away from everything and everyone in our lives must be just as strong as our attraction to them. Attraction must be balanced by the ability to let go, or we will lose ourselves to pleasure and never attain joy. This is the most difficult of all spiritual practices, and the most dangerous. How many of us are strong enough to dip into the pleasures of life and enjoy them without becoming attached to them? Don't we all know people who have destroyed themselves by drowning in wealth, power, sex, or drugs?

LIKE MERCURY THROUGH DUST

Have you ever broken a thermometer and watched the mercury fall to the ground and bead up? It rolls around in tiny balls of silver, yet nothing it touches adheres to it. This, the spiritual masters of the East tell us, is how we should try to live our lives—like mercury through dust, clinging to nothing.

If we can find ways to practice non-attachment now, while we are living, we will be that much more able to let go of the world and the people we love when the time comes. There are actually simple and intriguing exercises in non-attachment that we can practice.

- Find the richest chocolate or other favorite dessert of yours and take one bite. Only one bite. Then give it to someone else to eat.

- Go through your closet and find your favorite shirt or dress. Take it downtown and give it to a stranger or drop it off at a Goodwill store.

- The next time a rude driver tries to cut in front of you in traffic, slow down and let him.

You will be amazed at how easily you forget that dessert or that favorite piece of clothing. You'll find that in a few days you have put it completely out of your mind, proving to yourself that you can live without it. When not fighting other drivers on the road, you will notice that driving becomes more enjoyable. Your stress level drops, and you feel calmer and more in control behind the wheel. You begin to see other motorists scurrying around in a big hurry to get nowhere.

Practice these exercises in non-attachment regularly and any others you might think of. Notice whether you long for the object you have given away. If you do, repeat the exercise from time to time until your desire for those things is balanced by the ability to let go of them.

Eventually, of course, we will let go; we will have no choice. Death will come, take us by the hand, and either gently lead us out of this life or drag us out kicking and screaming. Either way, we will let go. How much more peaceful that dying process will be if we have practiced some non-attachment during our lifetimes. And how much easier it will be for those left behind to see us die in tranquility rather than struggling against the inevitable.

Like the wisdom of *The Tibetan Book of the Dead*, the greatest benefit of the practice of non-attachment is the wisdom it imparts for living our lives. When we go through life non-attached, we are less likely to quarrel over differences of opinions, for we are not attached to winning. We give our orchestra seats to two starry-eyed young people who have never been to the theater in exchange for their balcony tickets. Having practiced non-attachment, we are no longer attached to having the best seats in the house. We allow our children to make their own mistakes and learn their lessons from experience because we are attached neither to showing how wise we are nor to leading them down the path we want them to follow. We allow other drivers to cut in front of us even when they are rude about it, because we are no longer attached to being the first or the fastest; neither are we attached to "teaching people a lesson" by speeding up and not letting them cut in.

Non-attachment, difficult as it is, allows us to find some modicum of contentment in our lives. It also leads us to the discovery that often, when we are strongly attached to something, it turns out that our attachment is not about the thing we're attached to but has more to do with something deep inside ourselves: a longing to feel loved, a feeling of being incomplete, our sense of inadequacy. It's never about what it's about.

CHAPTER ELEVEN

CONFUSING THE EXPERIENCE WITH ITS OBJECT:
DISTINGUISHING THE INNER AND OUTER WORLDS

I've been thinking about this chapter for several days, wondering exactly how I would discuss this topic and worrying about finding an example to use. I was on my way to go jogging in Golden Gate Park this morning but stopped for just five minutes at the post office to pick up some postage stamps for Paul because he was going to pay bills in the afternoon and was out of stamps. I checked the writing on the green curb to make sure it was legal to park there. It said it was a ten-minute parking zone, so I ran in, got my stamps, and came right back out, only to find a meter monster writing me a ticket.

I protested loudly, pointing at the curb and the "10-Minute Parking" notice, to which the meter monster responded by pointing to a sign I hadn't seen. From noon until 2 o'clock on Thursdays it was a "no-parking" zone so the street sweepers could come by and clean the gutters. I pointed out how illogical it was to have the same stretch of curb be both a ten-minute zone and a no-parking zone at the same time. I pleaded as he kept writing. The meter monster jockeyed his Cushman cart up next to me, thrust the ticket into my hand, and smugly said, "Here you go."

Then he drove a few yards ahead and began writing another ticket. I was furious.

I sped away to the park and ran an intense mile and a half, plotting all the while how I would get even. This is what I did:

- First I went home, got a carbon steel knife, sharpened it, and went looking for the meter monster. When I found him, I followed on foot as he made his way from car to car. At one point, he had to get out of the Cushman and walk up a short incline to read a license plate. When he did, I slipped up quietly and slashed both back tires on his Cushman cart, then slunk away unnoticed.

- I found the meter monster elsewhere in the neighborhood writing out a ticket. I pulled up next to him in my truck and put down the passenger window. He looked up. "Excuse me," I said. "Why are you meter guys so fat? Don't you ever haul your asses out of those stupid golf carts and walk once in a while?" I could see the fury in his eyes. He started to say something, but I laughed, put up the window, and sped away.

- I followed the meter monster home that evening, and after he went into his nice suburban house, I spray painted his Oldsmobile with red paint.

- I sneaked up to the meter monster's house in the middle of the night with a can of black paint and wrote across the front of it in bold letters: "A curse! Your children will grow up to hate you."

• I went home, got my baseball bat, found the meter monster, and beat him until he begged for mercy.

Of course, I did all these things only in my imagination as I jogged around the soccer field, but it felt great. Paul and I do, however, keep a baseball bat and punching bag in the garage for just such occasions, and when I returned home from my run, I had a cathartic five minutes beating the hell out of that punching bag.

It is a healthy sign that I can act out my rage in fantasy and not on the person himself. This is always much better than lashing out and hurting someone. It is also better than attempting to "stuff" such enormous feelings inside and hope they'll go away on their own.

How kind of the Universal Consciousness to provide me with such a potent example to use in writing this chapter—and for only the 25 dollars it will cost me to pay the ticket!

What exactly was going on in this situation? Was my response—wanting to beat the man's brains in, for example—a reasonable response to being given a parking ticket? I think not, especially since I had parked right next to the sign posting the no-parking hours. It was, after all, my own fault for looking down at the curb but not thinking to look up for signs on poles.

It didn't take long to figure out what buttons had been pushed. My authority/father figure button, for one. I was being made to feel insignificant by being ignored as I pleaded for mercy. I was being disrespectfully rejected as my logical arguments against having a ten-minute parking zone and a no-parking zone in the same spot were being ignored, if not scoffed at. I was being insulted by having the ticket thrust haughtily into my hands. Then this infuriating authority figure drove off, as though I wasn't even deserving of a response. I was feeling invisible and persecuted, the same way I have felt in the past when being treated badly for being gay or for having HIV disease, and it was coming from an authority figure, a Bad Father figure.

Lots of buttons were being pushed, all right. And it was very clear in my mind who was at fault: the fat, mean, ugly meter monster. It was all about him. He was the cause of all my woes, and I was convinced that eliminating him, or at least making him suffer, was the solution. Luckily, I worked out most of my feelings before Paul returned home that afternoon; otherwise, we surely would have had a horrible fight over something ridiculous and completely unrelated.

What I was doing, of course, was confusing the experience I was having with the object that triggered the experience. I wanted to kill the meter monster. I was fixated on the man "out there," the "object" in the outer world. He started it; he made it happen; he was the reason my day was ruined.

Well, all of that is partially true. He did start it insofar as he was the trigger, the catalyst. When he wrote me the ticket, lots of feelings inside got activated. At that moment my pleasant morning took a nasty turn. My experience went from being content and happy to being agitated and angry. So I did what most, if not all, humans do: I focused on the object of the experience—the meter cop—rather than the subject of the experience—me.

That is an understandable reaction, and one could even make an argument for pursuing this individual. Perhaps I could appeal the ticket. I fantasized having the ticket thrown out and even having the meter cop disciplined. But all that energy was directed in the wrong place. The experience was in me, not in the outside world. It wasn't the meter guy who was having my experience. He was having his own experience. I needed to address the experience, not the object of the experience. I needed to address what was going on inside me.

One way was to act out in fantasy all my vengeance, which I did as I jogged that morning. The physical activity also helped me get rid of the palpable energy that had built up under all those feelings. When I finally calmed down I was able to explain to myself that, objectively speaking, I got the ticket because I parked where I was distinctly instructed not to park. Had I been across the street watching someone else get that ticket I would have sympathized, but I also would have thought, "Too bad the guy didn't look around and read all the signs before he parked there."

Of course, I knew all this was really about something else. I knew by the strength of my feelings that buttons were being pushed from a long time ago, buttons that had lots to do with other things in my life and not much at all to do with getting a parking ticket. It's never about what it's about.

A while back I was working on a novel, which was taking up lots of my time. During that period Paul decided to devote extra energy to his body. He developed a really strenuous exercise regimen at the gym to try to get his body in the kind of shape he has always wanted. He decided it would be a kind of individuation exercise, a way to accomplish something he had been told his entire life by his biological family that he could never achieve. As a child, he was derided for being overweight. As an adult, he is in excellent condition, but he wanted to push it to the limit and see if he could make his body exceptional. He thought of it as a spiritual exercise, a kind of hatha yoga. He would enter into this project prayerfully. Also, of course, it would occupy him during my long writing sessions. I encouraged him.

In the course of his working out, he met people at the gym. One of them was a fellow of whom Paul spoke highly. The two of them became friendly and would have lunch together, talk on the phone, work out at the gym together. One day Paul brought home a photo of the guy, which he put on his desk. The photo confirmed my worst suspicions: This guy was gorgeous. He had a beautifully developed body, a handsome face—the works. Paul had previously told me how intelligent the guy was and that he had expressed an interest in talking with Paul about developing himself spiritually. This made me nervous.

In the past I have lost two boyfriends to other men. Both times they were men my boyfriends met at the gym, and both times the guys were much more muscular and physically developed than I. Both experiences were extremely traumatic for me, given my huge personal issues around abandonment. So this new friendship was extremely threatening.

During the next two weeks Paul and I confronted this issue. I wasn't able to get my feelings under control and it seemed no amount of reasoning was working. I was sure that this was the beginning of the end of our relationship. He tried everything to reassure me, but nothing worked until one morning when I asked him at least to admit that he was infatuated with this guy.

He smiled slightly and said, "Honey, I'm infatuated with somebody every day. But I understand that the infatuation is about me, not the person I'm infatuated with. My infatuation begins in me and ends in me. Whenever this happens I ask myself, 'What is going on inside me that I am having this reaction to that person?' I know it's never about what's on the outside. It's always something in me, and that's where I try to solve the issue. I would never be so foolish as to allow something like that to jeopardize my home and my relationship with you. I just wouldn't."

I responded by saying, "But you could easily be swept completely away by your feelings and not be thinking clearly."

Paul laughed out loud, pointed his finger at me, and replied, "No, honey. You could easily be swept completely away by your feelings and not be thinking clearly. I don't work that way. I get swept away by my mind. That's an entirely different set of problems. You have one way of approaching life; I have another."

I immediately began to feel calmer. Yes, that inner voice said. This felt true. I was projecting my way of reacting to the world onto Paul. Not only that, but I had quite completely confused the experience I was having—terror at being abandoned—with the object which triggered it—Paul's new acquaintance at the gym. My experience was going on in me. Paul's gym buddy was out there in the world having his own experience of life and probably has never even thought about me or any of the things I am afraid will happen.

ALL MY EXPERIENCES BEGIN AND END IN ME

Have you ever been to an amusement park and watched people on a roller coaster? Some people are terrified just waiting in line. They hop back and forth from foot to foot and chatter non-stop with whomever will listen. Others appear quite calm. They stand virtually expressionless, watching the roller coaster car climb the tracks, plummet down and around, jerk, and begin to climb again. Some people are laughing; others look as though they are about to cry.

When it is their turn to ride, the group gets into the roller coaster car and again, some are absolutely frantic with anxiety while others are slow, calm, and methodical. They even think to straighten their skirts or remove their hats before the ride starts. When the group begins the ride, their faces are either placid and calm or contorted in excitement. As they begin to ascend the first steep incline, some riders chatter, some are silent, still others are already beginning to scream. When they go hurling over that first crest and speed downward, the shouts can be heard all over the amusement park. Yet a few of the riders still sit calmly, not making a sound.

It's always intriguing to watch as the roller coaster comes gliding back to the loading ramp. People's faces tell the whole story of their experience. Hair is wild and wind-blown, cheeks are flushed, some of the more frightened people are crying; others are laughing wildly. And there are still a few whose eyes are filled with excitement but who appear calm and collected.

Every once in a while, you find people who will ride the roller coaster over and over again. They hop out and get immediately in line to ride again. By their fifth or sixth ride, they seem completely at ease. They have become used to the thrill of the roller coaster and now it is no more exciting than a car ride to the nearest supermarket.

The roller coaster itself never changes. It is simply a mechanical device that rolls an open car up and down a long, curved track. Everyone who gets aboard takes the exact same ride. Yet each person has a separate experience. For some, it is so frightening they will never do it again. For others who have ridden it before, it has lost its thrill, and they go looking for another, more stimulating ride. For still others, it is absolutely exhilarating, and they can't get enough of it. Then there are those who never found it thrilling to begin with. For whatever reason, some people seem inured to such dangers and excitements.

Each experience in each individual is completely unique. Each experience begins in each individual as he or she climbs aboard the roller coaster and ends in each individual as he or she climbs out when it is over. The object of the experience—the roller coaster itself—remains constant. The subject of the experience—each individual person—is unique, and therefore each experience is unique. To confuse them would be unreasonable and possibly even dangerous. Yet it happens all the time. People often confuse their experience with the object that triggers the experience. When that happens, all sorts of problems arise.

Imagine if every person who rode the roller coaster in terror went running to the authorities and tried to have the roller coaster closed down because it is "a terrifying and dangerous thing." Silly, you think; no one would do such a thing. But that is simply not so. Such things happen all the time. A person reads a book and finds it offensive for any number of reasons. He is embarrassed by the sexual frankness of the narrative. He finds the philosophy of the author insulting to his religion. He is angered by the liberal use of expletives in the characters' dialogue. Immediately, this reader begins a petition to have the book banned from the local library. We read of this happening almost every day.

Mary has been jilted by her boyfriend, Frank. She feels unloved, rejected, even abandoned. She stops dating men for the rest of her life. A young boy eats three chocolate bars and goes to bed. That night, he has horrible nightmares and wakes his parents several times. His parents decide their son can never eat chocolate again and refuse to allow it in the house. Freddie goes to a movie which turns out to be quite poignant and sad. He cries at the end, and one of his friends teases him about it. From that day on, he reads the movie reviews of every film he considers seeing to find out if it is sad. If it is, he refuses to see it.

Almost every day of our lives each of us at some point will confuse the experience we are having with the object which triggers it. The fact is, the experience is in us. It begins in us, just like the roller coaster ride begins when we climb in and the car starts moving; and it ends in us, just like the roller coaster car glides to its slow, even stop. To address our experience by focusing our attention outside ourselves is to miss the point entirely and never truly to address our real issues.

Look at our two original examples. True, the meter monster who gave me the parking ticket infuriated me by doing so. If he hadn't given me the ticket, I wouldn't have become so enraged. But the anger, regardless of who instigated it, was in me. Only by going inside and confronting the experience inside myself can I ever understand it. Nothing I possibly could do to the meter person would change that experience. I might supplant it with another experience, say, one of satisfaction at having sought my revenge, but that would not be getting at the real issue. That would simply be covering over one experience with another. It would be similar to spraying a sweet-smelling room deodorizer over a foul smell in the air that is caused by rotting garbage. It will last for a while, but when the spray evaporates, the foul smell will still be there because the cause of the smell is still there. So it is with some of our experiences, like the one with the parking ticket.

The only way for me to address the intense anger that getting the ticket stirred up in me was to "go inside" and find out why I got so angry. We can almost always be sure that it will have little or nothing to do with the actual triggering object or event. It's never about what it's about.

Regardless of whether I talked Paul into never seeing or speaking to his friend again, the real cause of my experience was deep inside me. If I don't get at the feelings which were being triggered in that situation, I am doomed to repeat it. When Paul pointed out that he was fully aware that all his infatuations are inside him and have nothing to do with any person he might become infatuated with, he showed me the way to stop dwelling on the object which had caused my strong emotions. Only then could I begin to look at what was really going on inside me. By getting at my own fears of rejection and abandonment, where they came from, and which of my inner selves was carrying those feelings, I could begin to manage them better.

When we address the object of our experience (the outer world) rather than the experience itself (the inner world), we remain doomed to repeat the experience over and over and to be racked with pain and suffering. Until we pay attention to the source of the feelings rather than to the object which triggers the feelings, we are confined to an emotional prison.

People like focusing on the object because it is easier. It is always much easier to find the person who gave me the parking ticket and slash his tires or hurl insults at him than it is to grapple with myself for days or weeks as I try to get at my deep inner world. It is much easier on my ego to blame Paul for causing my jealousy than to reflect on myself and determine why I have feelings of jealousy or envy in the first place. When I am introspective and discover why I think, feel, and behave in certain disturbing ways, I must then find some course of action to address those feelings, thoughts, and actions so I can better manage them. That is a lot of work.

I certainly don't look forward to the grueling task of self-examination and introspection, dredging up the source of my discomfort. And once I identify the feelings and their source, then I have to take on the real work, the work of finding a way to handle the feelings now and in the future. It would be much easier, at least in the short run, to blame Paul and his friend for all my torment and to make it Paul's responsibility to "fix me" by not seeing his friend again.

But all fixes that focus on the outside are temporary. Shouting at the meter monster or making Paul miserable until he ends his friendship or stops going to the gym altogether will just put a Band-Aid on an open wound. Sooner or later it will start bleeding again, and I will be right back where I started.

The only answer to understanding our inner experiences is to go inside ourselves, which is where all experiences begin and end. That's where we will learn the secrets of managing our feelings, whether they are terrifying or exhilarating. We must learn not to focus on the object in the outer world. That is just an image, a trigger. It is not the true cause of our distress.

CHAPTER TWELVE

THE WORLD IS A TAR BABY

There is a series of children's stories set in the deep South of the United States known as "the Uncle Remus Tales." These fables, told by a wise old African-American man, center on a cast of colorful animal characters who are always fighting with one another. The perennial conflict at the heart of the stories is between Brother Fox—or Br'er Fox, as it is said in that part of the country—and Br'er Rabbit. Br'er Fox is always trying to find a way to catch Br'er Rabbit and put him in a stew. But Br'er Rabbit is way too clever for Br'er Fox and is forever slipping through his grasp, always "outfoxing" him.

One of the most famous tales tells of the time Br'er Fox sets up a tar baby in the road. He makes a figure out of warm tar, dresses it in a coat and a hat, and waits in the nearby bushes for Br'er Rabbit to come hopping along. Eventually, Br'er Rabbit passes by. Seeing this figure in the road and being the amiable fellow that Br'er Rabbit is, he stops to chat with the tar baby. But the tar baby, of course, doesn't talk back. The more Br'er Rabbit tries to engage the tar baby in conversation with no success, the madder he gets. Finally he threatens the tar baby. "Either you say something, or I'm gonna punch you in the nose." And so Br'er Rabbit is forced to punch the tar baby for not being polite and passing the time of day with him.

As planned, when Br'er Rabbit hauls off and lands a punch in the tar baby's face, his hand gets stuck in the tar. He tries to pull it out, but it will not budge. He pushes on the tar baby with his free hand, and that hand also gets stuck. Next, he puts his right foot up on the tar baby's chest, trying to pull himself free, and of course, that too gets stuck. Soon Br'er Rabbit is exhausted and hopelessly stuck in the tar baby. At that moment Br'er Fox and his cohort, Br'er Bear, come ambling out of the bushes. "Well, well, what have we here?" Br'er Fox says, and at long last, he has caught himself the makings for rabbit stew. (Never fear, Br'er Rabbit escapes this predicament in the end.)

Had Br'er Rabbit been able to resist punching the tar baby, he would not have gotten himself in such a predicament. Had he been able to manage his outrage, he would have remained safe. Had he been able to resist the urge to engage the tar baby at all, none of this ever would have happened.

THE TAR BABY OF DESIRE

I often think of this tale when I find I have engaged the world just a little bit and ended up embroiled in a thick and worrisome dilemma. I once had a fine old Dodge that was a bit of a clunker but ran just fine. I knew whenever I got into that old car I would get wherever I was going, even if I didn't arrive in a grand style. As I earned a little more money in my career and began seeing myself as a "professional," I also started fancying myself a man-about-town. I wanted to be seen by others as prominent, successful, and devil-may-care. So I traded my old jalopy for a flashy new red convertible.

For the first few months I was in bachelor heaven. I drove around town with the top down, even in cold weather. People would turn and stare at me in my shiny new car. Men would flirt with me. Women would flirt with me. Other drivers craned their necks in envy as I passed them on the highway. I was as proud of myself as I had ever been. My ego was inflated to the size of a blimp.

About a year after buying the car the clutch began slipping. After that the transmission went out. Then the electrical system. For as long as I owned that car, it gave me nothing but trouble. The car spent as much time in the shop as it did in my garage. And I was not only paying for the repairs, but I also still owed money on the car.

I think of that car as a red tar baby. Had I not been tempted by "the world and its charms," had I been content and secure in myself and not felt I needed the envy of others, I would never have ended up spending so much time and money on a car that never worked properly. I could have devoted that time and energy to other, more rewarding things.

Once I saw that car, I had to test-drive it. That was like sticking my finger in the tar baby's chest. Once I test-drove it, I began collecting pictures and brochures. That was like sticking my whole fist in the tar baby. Then I went to the dealer, just to see what kind of a trade-in he would offer me for my old Dodge. That was like sticking my arms in up to the elbows. Then I actually let the dealer write up a sales agreement for me to think about for a few days. That was like sticking my feet in the tar baby's chest. As I ruminated for days, imagining what it would be like to pull up to my friends' houses in a shiny new convertible or meet someone at a bar and watch his face as I led him to my convertible to give him a ride home, I was tugging and pulling and getting hopelessly stuck in the tar baby of desire. By that time it was too late. Br'er Fox, in the form of desire, was already firing up the stew pot.

As long as I owned the car and kept putting money into it I was just getting more and more covered with tar. I had stuck my finger into the tar baby of desire when I went to the car dealer in the first place, and ever since, I had been grappling with the results. I had engaged with the material world, and I was paying the price for it—on many levels. It was costing me money, time, energy, and pride. I was frustrated, angry, and regretted having bought the car. Eventually, I sold it and bought myself a Toyota station wagon, which never once in ten years gave me a bit of trouble. But, of course, I bought the station wagon in order to have a practical mode of transportation, not to flatter my ego.

All the world is a tar baby, if you think about it. How many times have we engaged the world and been sorry afterward? It doesn't even have to be for dubious reasons. Every time I go out into traffic I am reminded that there is a price to pay for being in the world. If I want something from the world, I will indeed have to pay for it.

If I want to publish my writing, I must be willing to submit it and have it rejected dozens, if not hundreds, of times. That takes time and energy which I would normally spend writing something new. So I must then decide: do I want to write or do I want the world's approval of my writing by having someone publish it? Writing involves no one but me. Publishing involves the world of agents, publishers, public relations people, editors, critics, readers, accountants, and countless others. All of that takes me away from my writing.

Ego always thinks it can stick just one finger into the tar baby and let it go at that. By now you and I know better than that. I have no doubt that by the time you read this I will have had several more tar babies in my life.

GOOD TAR BABIES

Not all tar babies are bad, by any means. Many are genuinely positive and admirable activities to engage in. But we must always keep an eye on our motives. They can change without us being aware.

As mentioned earlier, I was appointed to a statewide working group on AIDS which does wonderful work setting up health care programs and distributing millions of dollars to serve people too poor to afford proper health care. The first year I belonged the group met three times in three parts of the state. At that time I was single, Andre having died the year before. Traveling around was no hardship at all.

I found myself getting quite involved in the working group and wanting to contribute to its success, so I began a newsletter, which I published quarterly. The majority of people on the working group are service providers and staff from government agencies. So during my third year on the group I formed a caucus of people with HIV to make sure the voice of people with AIDS was being heard. Last year the Governor asked us to devise a statewide plan for dealing with the epidemic over the next three to five years, and so we ended up meeting six times instead of three, forming committees, having teleconferences, and writing reports. I also began working on a novel. And by this time I was involved in a committed relationship with Paul. Suddenly, I realized I was stuck in the tar baby of good works.

I began to notice—rather, Paul began to point out—that I was spending more time away from home, less time with him, and less time writing. He also pointed out how dissatisfied and cranky I had become. I decided to cut back on my involvement with the group and began thinking of ways in which to do it. I would let go of the newsletter. I would step down as chair of my committee. I would pass the leadership of the caucus to another member. Six months later Paul pointed out that none of my good intentions to reduce my involvement had been carried out. I explained to him the reason for that: The group needed me. Without me, those things just wouldn't get done. We argued; I admitted he was right, and I set actual dates for cutting back my activities.

As you may have guessed, when the deadlines rolled around I was still in the thick of things. Now I was stuck in the tar baby of ego. I just couldn't let go because I was getting so much positive feedback from people about how important I was to the group. Once I realized how "stuck" I was and that my good works were no longer primarily about the good works but about my ego, I was actually able to begin to let go.

Those tar babies are pretty sticky, even the admirable ones. For months I told myself my inability to cut back was because so many people needed me. The truth is, it was all about self-gratification. Well, the truth is seldom kind. And, of course, it's never about what it's about.

CHAPTER THIRTEEN

THE TRUTH IS SELDOM KIND

There's a kind of half-joke we play in our home. When one of us comments on something uncomfortable that we're trying to confront within ourselves, someone in the household will comment, "The truth is seldom kind." I was complaining the other day that the scales must be wrong because I knew I couldn't possibly weigh what it said I did. Paul smiled as he passed me in the hall and said quite matter-of-factly, "The truth is seldom kind."

A few weeks ago, Paul hung up from talking to his younger brother in Guam, and he was in a foul mood. Finally he started talking about it. "Kenny had the nerve to say that I'm just like my older brother." Naturally I couldn't resist commenting, "The truth is seldom kind."

There are few words in this day and age that carry the impact of "AIDS" or "cancer." Ask anyone who has sat across from his or her doctor and heard the words, "I'm sorry, but the test came back positive. I'm afraid it's AIDS." Or, "I have some bad news. It's cancer." In the few seconds it takes to say those words, a person's life changes irrevocably and eternally. Once said, the words' effects are permanent. Nothing is ever the same again.

The news that you are going to die doesn't digest easily or quickly. My late partner took to his bed for three days after finding out he was HIV positive. I've had other friends who simply went into their favorite bar and virtually were never seen or heard from again, at least not in any recognizable condition. The inescapable news that one is truly mortal isn't news any of us wants to hear, but it is something we could all benefit from hearing, if we allow ourselves to actually hear it and take it in. Most of the people I know have changed for the better after receiving that dreaded news. Like many other truths, it has a way of assisting us to transform ourselves.

Generally speaking, if there's something you don't like hearing, then you probably need to hear it. If you take the message in and integrate it into your consciousness, you will most likely transform yourself into a fuller, stronger, more independent person living a more substantial and satisfying life.

My life is filled with messages that I absolutely hated hearing, whether they came from friends, enemies or from some apocryphal voice in my head:

• You are sexually attracted to men, not women.

• You have absolutely no talent at mathematics.

•You are failing all your classes and will not graduate from high school.

• You're fat.

• You're becoming a drug addict.

- He's playing you for a sucker.

- This is a meaningless, boring, dead-end job, and you will die an unhappy old man if you don't quit and find something else.

- The person you love most in the world is dying.

- The person you love most in the world is dead.

- I don't love you.

- I love someone else.

- I'm leaving you.

- You have AIDS and will die within the next two years.

Usually, the more you hate hearing something, the more likely it is that what you are hearing is true. How many times have we been told by a true friend—or by that little Jiminy Cricket voice in the back of our minds—that the person we're dating is really wrong for us? We know we're unhappy in the relationship, but we can't face the truth of it. It's simply more than we can cope with at the moment the news comes to us. But when would be a good time to hear such news? Probably never.

Why don't we like hearing the truth? Most of us proclaim loudly that we seek the truth and that we're not afraid of it. Yet when truth comes knocking at our door, we hide under the bed with a knife.

If we go back to our concept that we are made up of many inner selves, it might be easier to understand. It's not our entire self that doesn't like hearing the truth. It's our old friend ego who isn't thrilled with it. After all, news that hurts is always personal. It strikes at who we are, or, more precisely, at who we think we are. And that's ego's territory.

IN DEFENSE OF EGO

This is probably a good time to say a few words in ego's defense. One might get the idea from all that I've said that ego is an enemy rather than a friend. That is the farthest from the truth one could get. When it is in an enlightened state, as discussed in chapter four, ego is our best friend. Ego protects and defends the soul, stands guard over the Self. Ego allows us to have a clear and healthy image of who we are and what we hold valuable. Ego also, in its enlightened state, acts like an orchestra conductor, managing and leading all the inner selves in a harmonious mental and emotional concert of living. But like an orchestra conductor, Ego can be extremely sensitive, supremely temperamental, and highly defensive.

Ego doesn't like to be told it can't or shouldn't do things. Ego doesn't like to see itself as puffed up or wrong or engaged in shoddy thinking. When ego hears these messages, it immediately goes on the defensive, protecting itself in any way it can. So when ego hears something like, "I don't love you any more; I love someone else," imagine the defensive posture it takes. Suddenly, all love is thrown out the door. You decide you'll never love again. All men are vermin. Love is for the weak. You decide to devote the rest of your life to your professional success.

All of this is just ego taking a defensive posture. We say our ego has been "bruised." We talk about the need to go off and "lick our wounds." This is all ego, having her dress stepped on or being told his penis is too small. Most of the time it breeds either shame or embarrassment, and ego does not like to be ashamed or embarrassed. After all, that is not ego's job. Ego's job is to present to the world the strongest, happiest, smartest...well, that's what ego thinks its job is, anyway.

Ego, like yeast, if sweetened just a little bit, inflates and puffs up to ten times its normal size. When that happens, ego forgets that its primary job is to be in service of the Self. It begins to think its primary job is to serve itself. That's when we get into real trouble because that is when we least like to hear the truth, and it's when the truth is most likely to present itself.

When I got "too big for my britches" as a young boy, that's precisely when my mother would scold me and bring me "down a peg or two." As a young professional, when I thought my company couldn't possibly go on existing without me and I should be given whatever I asked for, that's usually when my boss would promote someone else instead of me. When I started going to the gym and developing my body and began to see myself as quite the attractive catch around town, that's exactly when my dates would turn off to my personality and go home early, then stop returning my phone calls.

LOVE, UNKIND TRUTHS, AND TRANSFORMATION

Ego doesn't like these messages, these "truths," and doesn't know what to do with them. If the cycle isn't broken in some informative and productive way, then ego goes on with the cycle of inflation and deflation with no possibility of change and no likelihood of transformation. So when someone who loves you delivers a message that carries with it the supplemental message that the truth is seldom kind and then stays around to help you cope with the truth, real growth is possible. That is usually when transformation begins from inflated ego to enlightened ego. It is also usually when love appears, because inflated egos repel people and enlightened egos attract people.

Someone once described true love this way: a lover gives to the beloved everything the beloved doesn't know or doesn't have that he/she is drawn to in the lover. The lover holds nothing back in order to control or manipulate or make the beloved dependent. True love is the exchange between two people of all the virtues and knowledge that the other doesn't possess so that when the inevitable separation comes, the surviving person will be whole, without the other person needing to be physically present.

So I teach my beloved to spell; he teaches me to balance the checkbook. I teach him how to bake bread; he teaches me how to garden. I teach him how to express his emotions more and not repress them; he teaches me how to use reason to control my emotions more and not to explode at the least provocation. We hold nothing back from each other. Holding back is what people often do because they fear that if they give the beloved everything, the beloved will abandon them when she has all she needs to live life on her own.

At some point unkind truths need to be faced and lived through. When the crisis is over, ego has the opportunity to see that it is still intact, still useful, still needed. Those unkind truths can help a person live a more meaningful life. Think of the people you know who had richer lives after their divorce. Often we

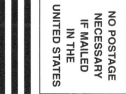

meet people who have blossomed professionally after being fired from a job they thought they would spend the rest of their lives at. It is quite common to hear people who have lived through terrifying disasters say that in the end it changed their lives for the better. Ironic but true.

Facing my terminal illness is not fun by any means. It is not a process I would wish on anyone. Yet at the same time, I strongly wish for everyone the transformative effect that this process is having on me. It allows me to appreciate life—each moment of life—in a way I have never even dreamed of before. There really is no way to achieve this kind of wisdom without going through the process of hearing and working through an entire warehouse of unkind truths.

If you have a true friend who will help, that is wonderful and probably the easiest way to develop an enlightened ego. But it can also be done through therapy, reading, meditation, keen observation, long contemplation. Gurus help their devotees to do this. Westerners have the wrong idea about Eastern spiritual masters. These gurus often say that the ego must be eliminated or destroyed. They don't mean that literally; they don't mean the ego must be killed. What they mean is that the ego must be transformed from an unenlightened stance to an enlightened one. Only in this way can it serve the soul, the Self, in the most helpful way. That means confronting the truth. And for ego, the truth is seldom kind.

CHAPTER FOURTEEN

RAGE, RAGE EVERYWHERE, BUT NOT
A VOICE TO SCREAM

"I abhor violence, but I adore rage." These words were spoken to me in a dream. There was no story, no series of events or images. I dreamt that I was sitting at my computer, writing, when a little man walked onto the page I was typing on the computer screen. He was wearing a blue suit and a black bowler hat, the kind you see in British films of the '40s and '50s. I understood this person to be me, or some part of me. He stepped up to the center of the screen, removed his hat, held it in his hands, and spoke directly to me. He said in a clear and distinct voice, not too loud but definitely not timid, "I abhor violence, but I adore rage."

He stood there for a moment, then replaced his hat, turned, and walked off the screen. I awoke immediately. This was obviously a message I needed to hear. Perhaps it was even one of those unkind truths I needed in order to understand myself better.

I thought long and hard about this dream and its distinct message. I also found it curious that the message should be delivered to me at my computer. What does rage have to do with my writing? Of course, it is always easier to see the trees in someone else's forest than in your own, but eventually I sorted it out.

My father expressed anger only twice that I can remember,

and both times I got a beating for something I thought was rather inconsequential. But his rage was extremely frightening to me because it became violent. I decided at an early age that I would never hit anyone when I was angry.

My mother, on the other hand, was always swearing, throwing things in the kitchen, and voicing her displeasures with life. Her tirades were seldom if ever directed at me, but her annoyance with life was a constant presence. It was also a small source of amusement for me. I found her quite intriguing when she vented her rage. She was so opposite from my father. She was never violent, and when she threw things, they never went flying at someone, which, in retrospect, I assume was deliberate. She just threw things to be throwing them. But it was clear she was enraged, angry at something or someone life had set in her path.

Most of the time I could tell she was just mad, not necessarily at any one thing or person, but at everything, at life in general. Life was difficult and frustrating, and she was going to acknowledge that frustration whenever she felt like it. But at the same time, you could see in her eyes that she was having a great time. I never remember her engaging in one of these temper tantrums without turning to me directly or shortly afterward and laughing. I guess that's where I learned that expressing feelings was a healthy thing to do on a regular basis. The place I tend to vent it most is in my writing, so what better place for this little man with the message to appear than on my computer screen?

WATCHING THE PRESSURE COOKER

Growing up with my mother throwing things on a daily basis and my father skulking around for months at a time and then exploding all over the place resulted in my formulating what I called the "pressure cooker theory of emotions." My observation of the people around me—virtually all the people around me— was that they treated their emotions like a neglected pressure cooker. It's as if someone read the instructions wrong. They thought the instructions said to tighten the lid of the pressure cooker, place it on the stove, and go about your business with no thought to when the fire should be turned off. After a while the pot explodes and the contents go splattering all over the walls, the floors, and any people who might be in the vicinity at the time.

I liked my mother's way better: let off a little steam all through the day. Swear at the jar lid that's stuck. Slap your thigh when you hear news you don't like. Sigh a lot. Talk to yourself. Curse in a foreign language; it's always easier when the people around you don't understand what you're saying. "Tsk" and shake your head at every annoyance.

You'll find that this method also works with other emotions. You will notice eventually that you are thanking people for the least courtesy, calling up strangers at the bank to tell them you appreciate the little favor they did you, giving people compliments, telling strangers how much you like their hair or blouse or even their smile. When you practice expressing your feelings, you begin to express all of them. Your inner selves become less tense, and therefore you become less tense.

One way to overcome the proscription about having your feelings, let alone expressing them, is to do some fantasizing, or imagining. I try to imagine that my feelings, particularly sadness and fear and rage, are actually people. I am sitting on the "sofa of my life," and they come along one by one and want to sit down on the sofa too. But, of course, I've given all the available room to Love,

Satisfaction, Happiness, and Contentment. I don't want any unpleasant feelings sitting next to me. I don't want Discomfort or Anger too close. Yet they too are part of the human experience. All feelings are valid; all feelings are worthy of being acknowledged. I must say "Yes," if not "Yes, please," to all of life. So I scoot over little by little and make room for them. That way they aren't looming over me or standing behind me, tapping their feet in irritated anticipation of when they're going to "get their turn."

I first learned to do this when, one after another, all my friends got sick and died. I found there was simply no way to avoid the feelings of sadness and anger and fear I was having. I tried for a long time to hide my feelings, even to ignore them, to pretend they weren't there. When I did that, the pressure cooker always exploded and always at the most inappropriate time. My sadness turned to depression, my anger turned to rage, and my fear became panic. But learning to carry them in my consciousness changed everything. It is never about avoiding, eliminating, repressing, or suppressing feelings. It is always about managing them, making them balance one another out.

All through my late partner Andre's illness, my therapist suggested I begin each day by crying a little. So I would. I would get up every morning, sit in the living room, listen to some music, and weep a little. I would often imagine I was holding "Krandy" in my lap, and we'd cry together. I would comfort myself, telling myself it was all right to cry and that I had every reason in the world to be sad. My friends were dead, my partner was dying, I was soon to be sick myself. Who in his right mind wouldn't be saddened by all of that? I would tell myself that I was going to go through the day feeling a little sad and a little joyful. I would carry sorrow in one hand, joy in the other, and try to balance it all out by staying conscious of all my feelings. I would try not to let them get the upper hand so that I lost control of myself, but I would acknowledge their presence throughout the day. I would try to make friends with them, all of them. From that time on, my feelings rarely careened out of control.

After Andre died I thought I would never stop grieving. And I didn't. But eventually I learned to live with my grief the way I learned to live with all of my other feelings. Grief, I discovered, is like a large round stone in your pocket that you can't get rid of. At first, it bothers you. It weighs down one side of your trousers, bangs against your leg when you walk, clunks on the chair when you sit down. But eventually you get used to it being there. You find yourself feeling for it, rubbing it, using it as a "touchstone" by which you measure things in life. Pretty soon you realize you would miss it if it disappeared. It doesn't. Grief never goes away; it just becomes something you learn to carry, like a smooth round stone in your pocket.

I often hear people say they have to "be strong," meaning they mustn't cry or show that they're having deep feelings about something. To my mind, that is the absolute opposite of strength. When a person has the ability to cry, to say, "I feel horrible" or "I can't stand it that you're sick and going to die" or "I am so angry at you that I'm leaving the room before I do and say things we'll both regret"—that takes true strength. Expressing the feelings that people around you are afraid to express takes monumental courage. The next time someone tells you to "be strong," say, "Thank you, I think I will," and weep uncontrollably on her shoulder right then and there.

ELIMINATE THE MIDDLEMAN

Another thing that living with my mother taught me, although I didn't realize it until I began dealing with AIDS, is that you don't need a "middleman" in order to express your feelings. You don't need someone to be angry at in order to be angry. Neither do you need someone to make you happy in order to be happy. These feelings can be experienced without being projected onto an external person. Yet this is the model we are constantly given in childhood. When anger is expressed in the home, it is always anger at someone. When someone in our family is happy, it is always because someone made him or her happy with a flower or a phone call or a card.

One of the most memorable Christmas mornings I ever had was the Christmas after my former wife and I separated. I was living alone in a big old flat in Washington, D.C., with my dalmatian, Dolores. It was a snowy winter, and my apartment seemed huge and dark and dreary. Two days before Christmas I looked at Dolores and thought it was unfair of me to make her go through Christmas feeling as bad as I did. I reminded myself that this divorce was something I wanted and that it was supposed to make me feel better, not worse. It had been five months since the divorce went through, and I had been moping about for the entire time. So I decided what more appropriate time to start feeling better than Christmas?

I went out and bought a Christmas tree. I had very little money, so I strung popcorn, made ornaments out of crepe paper and yarn and stuff from the corner thrift shop. I then went to Lord and Taylor and bought myself a beautiful vase in the shape of a lion's head. I had seen it a week before while shopping with a friend and had wanted it for the fireplace. It was expensive, and I couldn't afford it, and that is exactly why I did it. I was treating myself to something I would ordinarily never spend that much money on. I had it gift-wrapped and addressed the card to myself.

Then I went to the neighborhood pet store and bought Dolores toys and bones and wrapped those up as well.

Christmas morning, we sat in front of our Christmas tree and opened our presents together. Dolores lay enthusiastically chewing her presents as I sat sipping coffee and admiring the blue and white lion's head which now was sitting on the hearth with a big red poinsettia in it. Outside, it was snowing huge flakes. Across the street I could see a family through their living room window. They were happy and gay and tearing open their gifts. It was Christmas, and I was enjoying it with the being I loved most in the world, Dolores, and with the being I was learning to love most in the world, me.

I made myself happy that year, and it was probably the most purely happy I have ever been at Christmas. Later that day, while taking Dolores for a walk around the block, I found it ironic and sad to come across those same neighbors I had seen opening their presents earlier, outside fighting over who gave whom the better gift.

NONSPECIFIC ANGER

I learned through my partner Andre's dying process that it is quite normal and common to be "nonspecifically" angry, to be enraged at nothing visible, nothing concrete. There were times I wanted to kill—but not kill anyone, just kill as an indication of my rage and frustration at the illness that was robbing me of my loved ones. My rage was enormous. Thank God I had my writing to help me express it or I might have actually hit someone at the slightest provocation.

It is so common for me or Paul to be angry without being angry at a person or a thing that we have made up a code for each other so we will be aware that the other person is having "non-specific anger." One of us will go find the other and say, "I just want you to know I'm looking for a fight this morning." That lets the other person know that we're having strong feelings, usually anger, which we can't account for but which could get expressed at any moment. That way, if I snap at Paul, he will not take it personally. He'll know it's just me venting my nonspecific anger. On days like that I try to remember to go into the garage and spend a few minutes beating the punching bag with the baseball bat. Oh, does that place God in her heaven and make all right with the world!

Most of us walk around with lots of rage right beneath the surface. We're angry that we didn't get the life we wanted. Angry we married the wrong person. Angry we're in a dead-end job or our children or parents don't understand or accept us. And to make things worse, we're angry that we're angry and can't express it, because we were taught from childhood that it's not acceptable to express anger. No wonder people punch people who cut in line at the movies. No wonder motorists get out of their cars and shoot the person who bumped their fender. No wonder we're all so unhappy most of the time.

Next time you have even the slightest inkling you're angry, go find a pencil and break it in half. Or take a sheet of paper, wad it up and throw it as hard as you can against the wall. Do it as many times as you feel like it. You'll be absolutely amazed at how good it feels. It doesn't have to be a plate or a coffee mug; it's the "throwing as hard as you can" that is the release, not the smashing of things.

My friend Marjorie keeps a "screaming pillow" in her desk at work. Whenever she is having a particularly exasperating day she goes into her office, takes out the pillow, buries her face in it, and screams at the top of her lungs. She says it has enabled her to keep more than one job.

There are no bad feelings. There are only inappropriate responses to them. The most appropriate and healthy response to any emotion is to express it in some way that allows you to hold the feeling without hurting yourself or anyone else. That is what feelings are for: to have and to express. It's part of the human experience.

CHAPTER FIFTEEN

EVERYTHING YOU NEED IS WITHIN YOU

When my late partner Andre called his mother to tell her he had been diagnosed HIV-positive, she immediately responded by exclaiming to her only son, "Oh, no! And I was going to have a good year this year!"

He then went on to comfort her. When I asked him how he could be so calm when his mother reacted to his diagnosis of a terminal illness by making it all about her instead of about him, he simply answered, "I'm not buying into that. Do you think I want to be as miserable as she is?"

When my partner Paul's former landlord refused to refund his $1,000 security deposit, claiming he couldn't find the written agreement and had no recollection of ever receiving such a deposit, Paul walked away from the matter. I, on the other hand, was livid. "Don't you dare let him get away with that," I exclaimed. "Take him to court, make him pay."

"I'm doing what I think is right," Paul said. "I'm not going to let his bad behavior cause me to behave badly." Eventually his landlord did give him a check for several hundred dollars, but by that time the situation was so unsavory to Paul he signed the check over to an AIDS organization, refusing to keep money with that kind of energy attached to it. "I want to remain very clear about who I am and what I believe in," Paul told me. "That money came from an angry, hateful person out of a bad situation, and I don't believe any good can come from it so long as I have it."

Where do these people get this kind of character and determination? What is this attitude they have about themselves in relation to others?

I heard a story early on in the AIDS epidemic that has stayed with me to this day. There was a couple in the community who had been together for about five years when one of them, Bill, was diagnosed with AIDS and became ill very quickly. His partner, Raoul, was HIV negative, an activist in the Latino community, and healthy except for a kind of chronic hepatitis he had been dealing with most of his life.

Bill applied for Social Security disability, but before he did, he moved $7,000 dollars, his entire life savings, into Raoul's savings account so the government wouldn't find it and make him spend it all before giving him disability benefits. In those days practically no therapies or medications were covered by Medicare, and one bout of pneumonia could cost a person $10,000 just in uncovered medical bills.

At one point Bill went to spend a few days with friends who had a cabin near the Russian River. The evening he left town, Raoul woke up in the middle of the night with abdominal pains. A neighbor called an ambulance, and Raoul was admitted to the hospital, where, at 4 A.M. that morning, he died of acute hepatitic blood poisoning. Raoul's parents lived in the Central Valley and had stopped speaking to Raoul when he told them he was gay. Nevertheless, as "next of kin," that is, "blood" relatives, they were notified by the hospital administration of Raoul's death. They arrived the next morning, claimed the body, and arranged for it to be shipped back to Fresno for a funeral service. On Monday they hired a U-Haul truck, closed Raoul's bank accounts, and returned home.

By the time friends found out what had happened and notified Bill, everything was over. Bill returned to the city to find the apartment empty and all of his and Raoul's belongings gone. The money he had in his partner's savings account was gone, and their car had been taken as well. He telephoned Raoul's parents and tried to explain the situation, but they hung up on him. After that they refused to take or return his phone calls.

Bill eventually gave up trying to appeal to their sense of fairness and went to live with friends who took care of him until he died several months later. Various friends tried to get him to pursue legal avenues, but Bill refused, saying he did not want to spend what little time he had left in the frame of mind he would have to adopt to fight Raoul's parents. He said their attitude would be their own punishment and eventually it would turn back on them. (A year later a member of a women's motorcycle gang slipped on a wet spot in the family's supermarket and broke her hip. She sued the family for several million dollars and won.)

In the stories mentioned above, people decided for themselves that they would not allow someone else's behavior to dictate their own behavior. These people did not get stuck in the tar baby of revenge, nor did they confuse the object of their experience with the actual experience they were having. Instead, they insisted on following their own moral code rather than "fighting fire with fire."

On the other hand, I have seen people devoured by their

hunger for vengeance. I have watched people lie on their death beds worrying right up to the last minute about the money someone owed them, the injustice dealt them by the bureaucracy, the parent who disowned them when they announced they were gay. These people did not die peaceful, happy deaths. They died tortured by the need to make others see things their way.

Such is the strength of ego. Unable to put its agenda aside even in the face of death, ego will insist on being right, insist on being heard, and demand that the world give in. And instead of letting go of the human concepts of justice and vengeance, ego hangs on to its own agenda until we breathe our last breath. So we are imprisoned by the actions of others because we let their actions, no matter how dishonorable, determine ours. One of our inner selves takes over, and we must have vengeance. We are compelled to seek justice. We have to get even. Rather than let go of the situation and find our own inner peace, we must stubbornly try to change the outer world.

In the end, who wins in that kind of situation? We are tortured by anxiety, anger, and frustration until the situation is resolved. Sometimes that takes months or years. It can involve spending thousands of dollars in legal and court costs. Sometimes it just eats away at us. Often it is never resolved or is resolved in a way that makes us feel worse. Some people carry grudges and a hunger for revenge to their graves. My Uncle Ernie stopped speaking to a neighbor friend of his for 40 years because he wouldn't sell him an acre of land. He held that anger with him until the day he died. His ego simply couldn't accept another person's right to say no to him.

Likewise, however, enlightened ego is just as strong. An enlightened ego can turn away from the grossest injustice, feel compassion for the most ignorant and hurtful of foes, give up its agenda in the higher interests of the Self. At the last moment of our lives, which of these attitudes do we want? To die screaming at the world for not doing things our way, or to lie peacefully holding the hands of those we love?

Since our experience begins and ends in us and since the process of dying is, in the end, what dying is all about, wouldn't you prefer to spend your last few minutes in this life focused on what is happening at the moment rather than on what didn't happen over the past several years? We can do this only if we do not allow our behavior to be determined by the behavior of others.

WE ARE OUR OWN RESOURCE

Everything we need to live a happy, joyful life is in us, not in the world outside us. Somehow we have been made to believe otherwise. The movies, romance novels, myths that go uninterpreted for us and are taken at face value, all lead us to think that the power to make our lives complete lies somewhere in the world outside. Nothing could be further from the truth. If anything in life is true, it is that people, events, and especially "things" in the material world most often lead us to great unhappiness. It is only our attitudes toward those things that make us happy, and our attitudes come from within us.

When we put our hope in others to make us happy, we are begging for disappointment and heartache. No one can do that for us. We can marry the ideal mate, hold down the "perfect" job in the "perfect" company and work for the "perfect" boss. We might even have all the money we want. Yet if we are not content with our thoughts and our feelings, especially about ourselves, we will lead restless, even tortured lives.

The proof of our ability to determine our own happiness and success is with us at this very moment. Think of the last time you had an exhilarating dream. Perhaps you dreamed you were in love or flying above the earth or any number of fanciful dreams. Whatever the details of the dream were, you were blissfully happy. Yet when you woke you were in the same bed, in the same house or apartment where you live. Nothing in the outer world had changed at all. All the bliss you were feeling in your dream was taking place inside your own mind. You created the dream; you created the wonderful feeling.

Think of the worst nightmare you ever had. Perhaps you were being stalked by some monstrous villain or perhaps you were being murdered. Maybe you were being abandoned by someone you love. You woke in a sweat, shaking, maybe even screaming. Yet when you woke, you were in your own bed, in your own home, and nothing around you had changed one bit from the moment you fell asleep. All the horror you were feeling in your dream was taking place inside your own mind. You created the nightmare; you created the horror you were experiencing.

If we can do this in our dream states, we can also do it in our waking states. We are the authors of our lives, just as we are the authors of our dreams. The secret is in our attitudes, in the stance we take in our own lives. Remember what the great psychologist Viktor Frankl said: "We cannot always control the situation we are in, but we can always control our attitude toward it."

The most remarkable thing about the AIDS epidemic is that through all the horror and pain, the loss, fear, rage, intolerance, persecution, injustice, and grief, many, if not most of us, who live in the thick of it have been transformed. We have been changed into more enlightened people.

I would not wish upon anyone the deep sorrow I have experienced, yet I have never experienced such joy. I see life in general, and my life in particular, as an amazing, phenomenal experience. My undoing has been my salvation. I never would have looked so closely at my life, so deeply into my own psyche, so tenderly and vulnerably into my own heart, had those I loved and I myself not been dying.

I have looked deep into the heart of my pain and found reason and meaning in it. I have sat racked with sorrow at deathbed after deathbed and have willed the experience to mean something to me. I have learned and grown from each horror of this terrible epidemic. But make no mistake about it; not everyone will say that this has been his or her experience. Some people cannot or will not summon the courage to do the long, hard inner work. It is extremely painful, and we must try to have compassion for those who cannot engage their inner selves.

Viktor Frankl said we can will our lives to meaning. In fact, he said we must do so if our lives are to have any meaning at all. Meaning does not come from outside; it comes from within. I believe Frankl has the credentials to say such things not because he has a doctorate in psychology. His true credentials were not earned in the universities of Europe he attended but in the Nazi concentration camps. As longtime survivors of the AIDS epidemic, I believe Paul and I too have the credentials to speak with authority about such things. And we tell you with love and respect to find the meaning in your situation. Will meaning into your lives. It will not come to you any other way.

Looking back at my late partner's slow, agonizing death that dragged out over seven months, I realize only now that he was showing me how to face death with dignity and consciousness. Andre refused to take an abundance of pain medications. He took enough to stay comfortable but not so much that he was delirious. He always said he wanted to meet death fully conscious, head-on, face to face. He took emotional care of me during his illness as I took physical care of him. He talked about dying, talked about me surviving him. He fantasized with me about how I should spend his life insurance policy, urging me to travel, to buy myself a new car, to help others less fortunate. He listened to my woes and shared his with me. We tried very hard to stay conscious during those seven months of what precisely was unfolding before us: one of us was dying; one of us was not. There was about to be a painful tearing apart of a companionship built over ten years of being committed to each other.

Difficult as it may be to believe, he never complained. I have known many people who died slow, painful deaths who did not complain. I believe it was because they were acting as Boddhisattvas, showing the ones they loved how it is possible to go into your own death with grace, love, respect, and dignity. They were showing us that death is not an enemy but a wonderful friend who comes to take you out of this troubled place. Andre, my friend Pete, and my dear friend Elizabeth showed me how to let go of this world. I will use their example when my own time comes, and hope I can make my leaving as easy for Paul as they made theirs for me.

Understanding the meaning in Pete's and Andre's deaths did not come automatically or painlessly to me; nor did they interpret the experience for me. I discovered the meaning in those experiences by looking for it. I found it by looking closely at what was going on. Some of it I saw in the moment; some of it I saw in retrospect. But it was there all along. I had only to look for it.

I also had to look for it in my own diagnosis, in my own dying process. When I summoned the courage and looked very deeply, what I discovered was that even in dying, the principle holds true: it's never about what it's about. Smashing the mug when I trip over the dog isn't really about tripping over the dog; feeling stupid when my boss talks about my work isn't really about my boss; jealousy at my partner's new friends isn't really about my partner's new friends. And the lesson we learn from dying isn't really about dying. It is about living, about learning the value of life and how precious each moment truly is. It is about always asking, "Where is my ego in this situation?" And answering honestly.

It is about looking deeply into my relationships, keeping only the ones that mean something to me and working very hard at them. It is about seeking out truth in all its forms—pure and impure, holiness and horror—and looking truth straight in the eye. It is about comprehending that each second of my life that passes is a second that can never be lived again: Once time has passed, it is gone forever.

It's all up to us. In the end, everything is up to us. It is up to us in the beginning. It is up to us in the middle. And it is up to us in the end. We are our own resource. Just as we are the authors of our most horrifying nightmares and our most exhilarating dreams, so are we the authors of the meaning to our lives. The inner journey to find that meaning is the most exciting, frightening, profound, and joyful adventure we can undertake—if we have the courage to look in the emotional and spiritual mirror. Sometimes Paul and I are at a complete loss to identify where our courage came from, but we thank God for it every day of our lives.

Our hope, our wish in writing these things down, is that you, dear reader, will find your courage too.